>>>>>> Cinema One

21 Studies in Documentary

Studies in Documentary

Alan Lovell and Jim Hillier

The Viking Press
New York

The Cinema One series is published by
The Viking Press, Inc., in association with
Sight and Sound and the Education Department
of the British Film Institute.

Published in 1972 in a hardbound and paperbound
edition by
The Viking Press, Inc.
625 Madison Avenue, New York,
N.Y. 10022

SBN 670–67966–6 (hardbound)
    670–01954–2 (paperbound)

Library of Congress catalog card number: 72–75339

Printed and bound in Great Britain

Contents

Cover design based on a still from Diary for Timothy

48382

Foreword

The gaps at the level of both basic information and critical writing on the British cinema are so large as to make any discussion of it extremely difficult. There is no serious general history of the British cinema. There is also no full-scale account of the Rank Organisation, though Alan Wood's biography of Lord Rank has some useful information, or of the Associated British Picture Corporation, or British Lion. The only biography of Sir Alexander Korda is a short one. There is no sustained critical discussion of such important directors as Hitchcock (as a British film-maker), Carol Reed or Humphrey Jennings. The documentary movement (except in the writings of participants) and Ealing Films have been little explored or documented. Apart from a handful of useful books like Grierson's and Rotha's essays, Rachael Low's history of the early cinema and Sir Michael Balcon's autobiography, the critic is on his own in his attempts to understand the British cinema.

This means that discussion of the British cinema is inevitably superficial, with a few easy generalisations ('the British cinema is too literary', 'too class-bound', 'its directors lack talent') being endlessly repeated. We should be very foolish if we claimed that *Studies in Documentary* were likely to make any great impact on this situation. Three essays, in a book of this length, hardly allow for exploration in great depth. Our

7

aim has been to provoke serious thoughts about one of the most important aspects of the British cinema, the documentary tradition, by providing information and analysis of the ideas that guided the different manifestations of the tradition – thirties' documentary and Free Cinema – and by a close analysis of the work of one of the most distinguished documentary filmmakers, Humphrey Jennings. We can't claim to be comprehensive in our treatment of the three topics, but we have tried to approach them in a systematic and analytical way.

1: The Documentary Film Movement: John Grierson

Here is an art based on photographs, in which one factor is always, or nearly always, a thing observed. Yet a realist tradition in cinema has emerged only slowly. When Lumière turned his first historic strip of film, he did so with the fine careless rapture which attends the amateur effort today. The new moving camera was still for him a camera and an instrument to focus on the life about him. He shot his own workmen filing out of the factory and this first film was a 'documentary'. He went on as naturally to shoot the Lumière family, child complete. The cinema, it seemed for a moment, was about to fulfill its natural destiny of discovering mankind. It had everything for the task. It could get about, it could view reality with a new intimacy; and what more natural than that the recording of the real world should become its principal inspiration.

I remember how easily we accepted this in the tender years of the century when our local lady brought to our Scottish village the sensation of the first movies; and I imagine now it was long before the big towns like Edinburgh and Glasgow knew anything about them. These, too, were documentaries and the first film I saw was none other than Opus 2 in the history of the cinema – the Lumière boy eating his apple. Infant wonder may exaggerate the recollection but I will swear there was in it the close-up which was to be invented so many years later by D. W. Griffith. The significant thing to me now is that our elders accepted this cinema as essentially different from the theatre. Sin still, somehow, attached to play-acting, but, in this fresh new art of observation and reality, they saw no evil. I was confirmed in cinema at six because it had nothing to do with the theatre, and I have remained so confirmed. But the cinema has not. It was not quite so innocent as our Calvinist elders supposed. Hardly were the workmen out of the factory and the apple digested than it was taking a trip to the moon, and, only a year or two later, a trip in full colour to the devil. The scarlet women were in, and the high falsehood of trickwork and artifice was in, and reality and the first fine careless rapture were out.*

There is a popular misconception that John Grierson was a magician who created the British documentary movement out of thin air by miraculously persuading organisations such as the Empire Marketing Board and the GPO to make films. Grierson's achievement was remarkable by any standards but he was no magician. Something like the British documentary film would probably have emerged without Grierson's help. His special contribution was his acute reading of the situation and his ability, based on that reading, to determine a particular course of events, to exert influence on specific developments.

Grierson's contribution to the development of the documentary film was twofold. As a critic, theorist and producer he influenced the character of the films that were made. As an administrator and public official he helped create a commercial structure that made it possible for the films to be made and shown. Grierson's contribution was decisive, and it is necessary to discuss the development and impact of the documentary movement as a whole in the light of his ideas, but this inevitably means that some people who made an important contribution to the British documentary film are neglected here. In particular a full account would have to deal with Paul Rotha, director and producer as well as critic, historian and theorist of the cinema, whose contribution was just as varied as Grierson's.

Three key elements determined the situation out of which the

---

* *Grierson on Documentary* edited by H. Forsyth Hardy, Faber & Faber, London, 1966. All subsequent uncredited quotations are from this book.

British documentary film emerged. First, there was the development of mass political democracy and the consequent need to educate and inform the electorate, combined with the scepticism of some political thinkers about the possibility of this task ever being achieved. Second, there was the emergence of such media as the mass circulation press, cinema and radio, which provoked insistent public discussion of the impact they were having or were likely to have on democracy. Third, advertising and public relations were becoming recognised as important and growing sectors of modern society.

Grierson became preoccupied with these issues when he went to the United States in 1924 to study the formation of public opinion. While in America he became particularly interested in Walter Lippmann's critique of democracy (expressed in books like *Public Opinion*). Lippmann's pessimism about the working of democracy sprang from his belief that the ordinary voter could never make informed judgments because of his lack of relevant information and time for consideration. The starting point of Grierson's career was his acceptance of Lippmann's analysis. Intellectual conviction, however, was not enough for Grierson. He was determined to tackle the problems which concerned him and so change the situation.

That he chose the cinema as his instrument was in one sense accidental. Any of the mass media would have been suitable for the purposes he had in mind. Grierson says it depended on a chance remark of Lippmann's. He complained one day to Lippmann about the difficulties of research into the Press, and Lippmann suggested that the cinema might be more convenient to study since the basic data should be easy to get hold of. Grierson followed up the suggestion and went to Hollywood. There he met people like Walter Wanger, Chaplin, von Sternberg and von Stroheim, became actively interested in the cinema, and wrote film criticism for a number of American journals.

In fact his choice of the cinema was probably not as accidental as all that. For the 1920s saw a flowering of the cinema. The German Expressionist film, the Soviet film, American comedies and Westerns, and all the various experimental films provoked widespread intellectual interest. The use of the cinema for social and political purposes in the Soviet films was of great interest to Grierson, but he was even more responsive to the experiments in Robert Flaherty's films *Nanook of the North* and *Moana*.

When Grierson returned to Britain in 1927, he approached the Empire Marketing Board with the aim of putting into practice the ideas he had formed in the United States. If proof is needed that Grierson did not create the British documentary film out of thin air, the situation at the EMB at that time provides it. The Secretary of the Board, Sir Stephen Tallents, was very conscious of the need to publicise the Board's activities. The EMB was already using posters, newspapers and exhibitions, and was also interested in the cinema. It had given the Imperial Institute money so that it could arrange film shows for children. Rudyard Kipling had been approached to help in the making of a film, and although he refused, Walter Creighton was appointed Films Officer by the EMB as the result of a suggestion he made. Grierson enjoyed a sympathetic reception when he went to see Tallents – so sympathetic that he was appointed joint Films Officer with Creighton.

Grierson's activities at the EMB were varied. Undoubtedly, however, his most dramatic step was the making of a film, *Drifters*, which combined an approach derived from Flaherty, editing techniques suggested by Soviet films, and Grierson's own interest in a social process. At the same time Walter Creighton was at work on a film which was quite different in conception. *One Family* was a feature-length film (*Drifters* is 50 minutes long) meant to illustrate the story of the Empire and its economic interdependence through a whimsical tale in which Imperial cavalcades travel across the world to bring ingredients for the King's Christmas pudding.

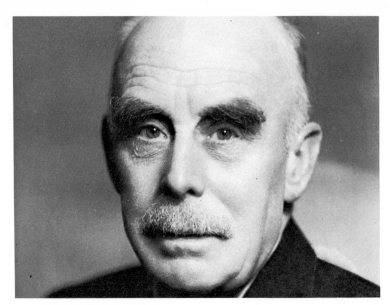

Sir Stephen Tallents

Drifters and *One Family* suggested two quite different ways of using the cinema as an instrument of propaganda. From the moment it was first shown in a programme of the London Film Society in the autumn of 1929, *Drifters* was accepted as the model for the propagandist use of the cinema. *One Family* was forgotten.

Films would have to be made on a regular basis if the working of democracy as analysed by Grierson was to be seriously changed. A source of finance was essential. Grierson's social philosophy, reinforced by the response he got from the EMB, naturally indicated State organisations as the most likely patrons; and throughout his career, most of his energies went into encouraging the State to support film-making. Finance became easier when large-scale private organisations followed the lead of the State. The Gramophone Company sponsored Arthur Elton's *Voice of the World*. Shell-

Alberto Cavalcanti

Mex and B.P. sponsored Rotha's *Contact*; the Orient Line, Rotha's *Shipyard*; the British Commercial Gas Association, Elton and Anstey's *Housing Problems*; the Southern Railway, Rotha's *Rising Tide*. In 1934 Shell set up its own full-time film unit.

When the EMB was closed down by the Government, Grierson and the film unit (along with Sir Stephen Tallents) transferred to the GPO. In the late 1930s he played an important part in the establishment of the National Film Board of Canada and gave advice to other Governments on the use of film. Ten years later he became Controller of the films section of the Central Office of Information. He had an important influence on the work of the Films of Scotland Committee, another State supported organisation. The only contact he had with the feature film industry was through the State when he was put in charge (along with John Baxter) of Group 3, the organisation set up by the National Film Finance Corporation to act as a training ground for young directors.

Possibly the most important work Grierson did at the EMB was the training of a group of film-makers. These film-makers became the mainstay of the British documentary film; they included Basil Wright, Arthur Elton, Stuart Legg, Edgar Anstey and Paul Rotha. The training was broad in conception; as well as technical expertise, it involved intensive discussion of the social and aesthetic ideas which Grierson was developing. The corporate spirit developed at the EMB became an essential part of the workings of the British documentary film. Cavalcanti described the situation at the GPO: 'The working conditions were similar to medieval artisanship; the work was collective, the films of each one were discussed.' (Quoted in *Quarterly of Film, Radio and Television*, Summer 1955.) The film-makers, not thinking of themselves simply as directors or individual artists, moved easily from directing films to producing them, to general administrative work and back again. Anstey took charge of the Shell Film Unit when it was first formed; Donald Taylor and Ralph Keene set up the Strand Film Company with Paul Rotha as the Director of Production; Basil Wright formed the Realist Film Unit.

Grierson's particular interest in the cinema as a method of social propaganda made it essential that the films should be seen by as wide an audience as possible. At first he concentrated on getting them shown commercially, and indeed throughout the 1930s British documentary films were shown in normal commercial cinema programmes. For example, the first six films made by the EMB (known as 'The Imperial Six') were sold to Gaumont British Distributors. However, commercial exhibitors were never enthusiastic about including documentaries in their programmes. So Grierson looked for other outlets. Noting that there was a potentially larger audience outside the commercial cinema than in it, he encouraged the growth of a non-theatrical audience, which included schools, film societies, YMCAs, various women's organisations, trade unions and many other bodies. The EMB set up a free loan film library for schools to service this audience; regular shows of EMB and GPO films were given at the Imperial Institute; both the GPO and the British Commercial Gas Organisation sent out vans to give shows on the road; and the GPO appointed an education officer to develop showings to the non-theatrical audiences.

The last part of the structure that Grierson helped to create was the critical magazines like *Cinema Quarterly* and *World Film News*. Although their interest in the cinema was not confined to the documentary film, these magazines had three important functions for the documentary movement. They were a convenient forum for discussing ideas – many of Grierson's essays were first published in their columns; they were useful instruments for publicising the work of the documentary film-makers; and they provided links with the film society movement (there were regular and detailed accounts of the activities of the film societies in both *Cinema Quarterly* and *World Film News*).

In helping to create this complex structure Grierson endowed the British cinema with a unique feature. He succeeded in linking the film culture (film as art) which had grown up in the late 1920s to an instrumental use of film (film as a medium for instruction, education, propaganda). Grierson captured or decisively influenced areas crucial to any film culture. First, through the film unit at the EMB he captured the young people who were actively interested in the cinema and who were likely to become film-makers or critics. It should be stressed that these young people were already interested in the cinema before they went to the EMB. Paul Rotha is a good example of this. Rotha's interest in the cinema was highly developed long before he worked with Grierson. He had attended the first performance of the London Film Society in 1925, he had worked for a short spell in the Art department of one of the commercial studios, and he had written *The Film Till Now*.

Second, a comparison of the critical magazines, *Cinema Quarterly* and *World Film News* with their predecessor, *Close Up*, shows clearly the impact of documentary ideas. Third, the ideas developed and the films made won the film societies for documentary.

The function of the documentary film

As we have seen, Grierson enthusiastically endorsed the kind of critique of democracy which Walter Lippmann had made:

That false assumption is the mystical democratic assumption that the citizen can be taught to understand what is going on about him, that he and his fellows in the mass can, through the electoral and parliamentary process, give an educational and rational guidance to the conduct of the state. . . . What we are trying to arrive at is the point where we abandon that purely mystical concept of democracy which encourages the illusion that ten million amateur thinkers talking themselves incompetently to death sound like music of the spheres. . . . We do not want people to know everything about everything all the time, because it is impossible. We do not want the people to make up their minds on specialised problems, because that is asking too much. We do not want to see them given as individuals a false notion of their freedom in society, and have them paralyse action with the infinite din of their amateur judgments. In particular we do not want to see encouraged a din in which the people's own best interest cannot be heard.

Lippmann was content to leave the situation as his analysis found it, with the ordinary citizen having no important part to play in political life, which would be dominated by experts. Grierson came to a different conclusion. He felt that such a situation would estrange the ordinary citizen from society and that this could only be damaging. Some way must be found of involving the citizen in his society:

We do want to see them given what they (the citizens) are not getting now: a service of information on the immediate needs and services of the state. We do want to see them given what they are not given

17

now: a living sense of what is going on. If we do not want to see their rational minds set impossible tasks we do want to see their sentiments and loyalties crystallised in forms which are useful to the people and to the State alike. Above all we want to see our society emancipated from its confusion and bewilderment, and given some imaginative leadership in the articulation of a faith.

The documentary film was Grierson's chosen instrument for this task. Its essential function was therefore an inspirational one. It might start by giving information about the modern world but its main function was to involve the citizen in the general social process.

It seems odd that the main aspiration of the British documentary film, which emerged in the 1930s when British society was persistently disrupted by social and political crises and gained a reputation for being politically radical, should have been not critical but inspirational. To understand this contradiction, some probing of Grierson's intellectual background is necessary.

Apart from frequent references to Walter Lippmann, Grierson does not give much indication of the ideas that helped to form his outlook. He neither develops his ideas consistently nor at such length that his intellectual position becomes clear.

The starting point of Grierson's position was a technological/collectivist account of modern society. According to this account, technological development, particularly in the field of communications, with inventions such as radio, cinema, the aeroplane, etc, was the decisive influence on modern society. Technological developments in communications made people throughout the world more aware of and more dependent on each other. Therefore the logic of modern society was collective organisation.

This account, with its emphasis on the effect of technology on the structure of society, has occasional marxist overtones. Grierson's identification of history as a force independent of men's wills also suggests a deterministic version of marxism.

He often insisted that if men are to act meaningfully they must move in the same direction as history:

But I emphasise the first and main point which is that we grasp the historical process and not bother about recriminations or moral strictures. Men are all the fools of history, even the greatest and best of them. . . . As educators we must go the way with history and men's needs, or others will come to take the privilege of education away from us.

But other strands in Grierson's position are quite unmarxist. He never refers to class and seems content with the existing hierarchical order of Society. The State, which is in no way seen as part of a class system, is identified with what best serves the long-term interests of people: 'The State is the machinery by which the best interests of the people are secured.'

It seems likely that Grierson's attitude was a combination of two different sets of ideas. The technological/collectivist emphasis probably came from sources like H. G. Wells, the Webbs and the Fabians. (Wells took an active interest in the British documentary films and Grierson describes how Wells was a regular attender at the London Film Society and had even said – in the GPO film theatre – that he was learning from the documentary film-makers.)

The other source is more difficult to identify. The idea of history as an independent force and the positive attitude towards the State suggest some kind of Hegelian influence. Indeed the more one examines Grierson's writings, the more likely it seems that he was influenced by neo-Hegelianism. Neo-Hegelianism, apart from reviving interest in Hegel in England in the later part of the 19th century, had been particularly concerned with the political role of the State, which it wanted to free from any notion that it existed to serve partisan interests. This belief in a strong, benevolent State is certainly

Basil Wright

present in Grierson. (If the identification of Grierson with the philosophy of F. H. Bradley, T. H. Green and Bernard Bosanquet seems an odd one, it should be said that Grierson studied philosophy at Glasgow University at the end of the First World War when neo-Hegelianism was still influential in British philosophy, and particularly so in Scotland – Bosanquet was professor of philosophy at St Andrews for a number of years.)

The contrast between Grierson's inspirational notion of the documentary film and the reputation it gained as a socially critical movement can be explained by a vagueness about the nature of the State that was characteristic of neo-Hegelianism. If the State was identified with the Government it could well have been argued that the British State in the 1930s did not represent men's interests and was actively opposed to the movement of history. But Grierson made an almost total separation between the State and politicians. He quoted Paul Valéry approvingly on this subject:

Political conflicts distort and disturb the people's sense of distinction between matters of importance and matters of urgency. What is vital is disguised by what is merely a matter of well being; the ulterior is disguised by the imminent; the badly needed by what is readily felt.

In so far as he identified the State at all concretely, he seems to have thought of it in terms of enlightenened bureaucratic organisations like the EMB, and public servants like Sir Stephen Tallents. The enthusiasm, generated by the films, for the work of organisations like these did not imply enthusiasm for all the Government's policies. Hence the position of the documentary movement in the 1930s vis-à-vis the Government was always a delicate one.

Grierson himself seems conscious of the problem that reliance on the State posed for the documentary film-maker:

It is important to note, however, that nothing can be expected from governments (as film sponsors) beyond what I shall call the degree of general sanction. The degree of general sanction is not the degree of sanction by the party in power: it is the degree of sanction allowed by all parties of Parliament or Congress.... I say as an old public servant that if the degree of general sanction is accurately gauged, maximum support is forthcoming for creative work. Where, however, advantage is taken and the degree of sanction is estimated on partisan lines, ineffectiveness and frustration result.

This, of course, imposes a clear limit on the creative artist working in the public service for, obviously, the degree of general sanction does not easily allow of forthright discussions on such highly controversial problems as, say, America's record with the Negroes in the South or Britain's record with the Indians in the East. The creative worker must not, however, simply denounce this limitation and dissociate himself from the government service. If he is a practical operator and a practical reformer he will take the situation for what it is and do his utmost within the limitations set, and this is one of the disciplines which the creative artist must learn in this particular period of society.

On the face of it this seems a sensible account from a liberal standpoint of the limitations of State sponsorship for film-making. But when looked at closely, it can be seen that Grierson's emphasis is not on the limitations but on the necessity of serving the State despite these limitations. Having made a plausible point about 'the degree of general sanction' he goes on to warn in headmasterly fashion about the dangers of trying to get outside the limits. 'Where, however, advantage is taken and the degree of sanction is estimated on partisan lines, ineffectiveness and frustration result.' Similarly, having described the large problems that a film-maker will not be allowed to deal with if he is sponsored by the state, he goes on to say that acceptance of this 'is one of the disciplines which the creative artist must learn in this particular period of society'.

The value Grierson placed on the State lays him open to the charge of being implicitly totalitarian. He was aware of this and tried to confront the issue: 'I am not going to pretend that I do not realise how "totalitarian" some of my conclusions seem, without the qualification I have just noted.' This qualification is an insistence that public guidance should be a two-way process: 'The government has as much information and guidance to get from the people as the people from the government.' But Grierson never indicated how the people were to make their views known to the government and he does not seem to have ever seriously thought about the problem. His emphasis was always on the effect the Government could have on the people:

Some of us came out of a highly disciplined religion and see no reason to fear discipline and self-denial. Some of us learned in a school of philosophy which taught that all was for the common good and nothing for oneself.

Paul Rotha

It is not, perhaps, surprising that a mixture of Calvinism and neo-Hegelianism should produce such an emphasis.

The nature of the British documentary film

So successfully did Grierson use the documentary film for propagandist purposes that it now seems the only kind of film that could have been used. But there do not seem to be good theoretical reasons for this, and a few films made in the 1930s indicate that other approaches could have been successful. Cavalcanti's *Pett and Pott* (made by the GPO Film Unit in 1934) is an example; it used a comic fictional story to publicise the social usefulness of the telephone. In opting for the documentary film Grierson was making a particular choice, a choice which he never really questioned and certainly never tried to justify at any length. In so far as he did discuss documentary he put forward a theory of 'naïve' realism along the lines which Siegfried Kracauer was later to develop at length in his book *Theory of the Film*. Grierson argued that the essential nature of the cinema came from its ability to record the appearances of everyday life (this for him was 'the real world'). Through its ability to record these appearances the cinema penetrates into the nature of that life. In his essay *First Principles of Documentary* Grierson put forward three principles:

1. We believe that the cinema's capacity for getting around, for observing and selecting from life itself can be exploited in a new and vital art form. . . .
2. We believe that the original (or native) actor and the original (or native) scene are better guides to a screen interpretation of the modern world. . . . They give it a power of interpretation over more complex and astonishing happenings in the real world than the studio mind can conjure up or the studio technician recreate.
3. We believe that the materials and the stories thus taken from the raw can be finer (more real in the philosophic sense) than the acted article . . .

The job of the film director was to come to know that reality.

. . . (documentary) must master its material on the spot, and come in intimacy to ordering it.

This one-page description of principles seems to be the nearest Grierson came to formulating aesthetic reasons for choosing the documentary mode. A variety of other reasons seem just as important as aesthetic ones. The practical one of cost was important; the documentary film was cheaper to make than the fiction films. Moral attitudes were also important. Grierson, a true child of Scottish Calvinism, was suspicious of dramatic fiction. He often refers to the fiction film in moral terms; 'meretricious' is a favourite description. He perceptively summed this situation up in a chance remark in his essay on the Films of Scotland Committee:

Several of the young directors responsible for the success of the British documentary film have been Scots; and there may even be some odd relation between the Knoxist background and a theory of cinema which throws overboard the meretricious trappings of the studio.

Any predisposition towards the documentary mode was likely to be encouraged in the cinema of the 1920s since the documentary film began to reassert itself at that time. Flaherty's films had the biggest impact on Grierson himself, but Cavalcanti's *Rien que les Heures* and Ruttmann's *Berlin* probably had a more general influence. To these should be added the Soviet cinema's general bias towards documentary, and particularly Soviet experiments like Dziga Vertov's *Kino Eye* and Turin's *Turksib*.

If the documentary film had been based only on a theory of naïve realism, it would have been close to the newsreel or the interest film. Grierson felt that his material had to be 'dramatised' or 'interpreted' if he was to achieve his ambition of using the film to involve men in the historical process. The impulse to dramatise the basic material was often in conflict with the principle of naïve realism but Grierson does not seem to have been consciously aware of the contradiction, except in so far as he favoured methods of dramatisation that were not too obtrusive.

The cinema of the 1920s offered three different methods of dramatising documentary material. First and most obvious there was the Soviet method of intense dramatisation (the use of stories and plots, the typing of character, rhetorical editing devices, etc). This was the obvious method to attract Grierson since the Soviet directors also saw the film as a social weapon. But in fact, Grierson does not seem to have been much attracted by Soviet techniques. The distrust bred by his Calvinist background for fiction and artifice was one reason for this lack of interest. More important seemed to be his ideological difference from the Soviet directors. He felt their methods of intense dramatisation were appropriate only to a revolutionary situation. But political revolutions were not the real stuff of the historical process for Grierson:

> The near relationship to purpose and theme is even more plainly evidenced by the great Russian directors. They too were begun in propaganda and were made by it: in the size of their story and the power of their style. One cannot do less when recording a world revolution than develop a tempo to take it. But the most interesting story of the Russian film does not begin until after *Potemkin* and *The End of St Petersburg*. These early films with their tales of war and sudden death provided relatively easy material, and did not diverge greatly in melodrama from the example of D. W. Griffith. There was the brighter cinematic style; there was the important creation of crowd character; but the whole effect was hectic and, in the last resort, romantic. In the first period of revolution the artists had not yet got down, like their neighbours, to themes of honest work; and it is remarkable how, after the first flush of exciting cinema, the Russian talent faded. Relating cinema to the less melodramatic problems of reconstruction was plainly a different matter.

This passage makes Grierson's social and political attitude very clear. Revolution is almost an irrelevance; work (which is abstracted from its social context) is the most important thing. Grierson makes his position even clearer a little later in the same essay:

> It is a commonplace of modern teaching that even with revolution, revolution has only begun. The Russian film directors do not seem to have appreciated the significance of this, for it would lead them to subject matter which, for the moment, they appear to avoid: to the common problems of everyday life and to the common – even instructional – solutions of them. But Russian directors are too bound up – too aesthetically vain – in what they call their 'play films' to contribute to Russia's instructional cinema.

Grierson's confident judgment on the Soviet directors proved to be very close to Zhdanov's under Stalin:

Sir Arthur Elton

They have, indeed, suffered greatly from the freedom given to artists in a first uncritical movement of revolutionary enthusiasm, for they have tended to isolate themselves more and more in private impression and private performance. . . . For the future, one may leave them safely to the consideration of the Central Committee.

The other possible methods of dramatisation were provided by Flaherty and the school represented by Cavalcanti's *Rien que les Heures* and Ruttmann's *Berlin*. Flaherty's method was to dramatise his films around a simple story. Grierson was hostile to this method because Flaherty's stories were associated with a romantic view of the world which he felt to be outmoded. From Grierson's point of view, *Berlin* and *Rien que les Heures* were the most suitable exemplars. Both films followed the lives of cities through one particular day. By editing together shots of events whose only common factor was that they occurred at the same time, they provided a cross-section of city life and broke away from being a simple narrative of events. The method had enormous influence on young film-makers of the time. But Grierson had one great objection to it. Cavalcanti and Ruttmann conceived their films as artists not propagandists. Their editing techniques were directed towards creating abstract, symphonic patterns. Grierson spent a good deal of time combating film-making of this kind, with *Berlin* as his special target.

Grierson finally chose the narrative account of particular social processes as his basic method of dramatising the subject of a film. *Drifters*, for example, follows the process of men catching fish, starting with the men on shore, following them out to sea and then returning to see the fish sold and disposed of; similarly *Night Mail* follows the mail train on its journey from London to Scotland; *Aero Engine* straightforwardly follows the construction of an aero engine. Inside the narrative of the films, particular emphasis was given to editing, using techniques derived from the Soviet Cinema.

Sound had a particularly important place in the aesthetic of the British documentary film. The documentary movement, developing at the same time as sound came into the cinema, was almost compelled to pay great attention to it. But the inflexibility and cumbersomeness of sound equipment made it difficult to use on location and forced the documentary film-makers to think very carefully about the use to which they would put it. Grierson devoted a complete essay to the subject, in which he followed the orthodox avant-garde line that sound should not simply be used naturalistically. Indeed, the documentary film movement became a laboratory for experiments in the non-naturalistic use of sound. *Night Mail* used poetry on the sound track; *Pett and Pott* replaced the natural sound of train wheels with recitative; *Coalface* used a chanting chorus; and numerous films dissociated picture and sound track by combining shots of one event with the sounds of another. Experiments of this kind drew artists like Benjamin Britten and W. H. Auden into the documentary film movement.

The British documentary film, then, can be defined in terms of a meeting between the cinema's recording potential (its ability to reproduce the surface phenomena of everyday life), various aesthetic devices developed by the film-makers of the 1920s and 30s (principally associational editing of picture and sound), and a technocratic/collectivist ideology. The ideological element is often thought to be the dominant one which determined a relationship in which aesthetic means were put at the service of ideological ends. In his later writings Grierson describes the relationship in this way:

Documentary was from the beginning ... an 'anti-aesthetic' movement. ... What confuses the history is that we had always the good sense to use the aesthetes. We did so because we liked them and we needed them. It was, paradoxically, with the first rate aesthetic help of people like Flaherty and Cavalcanti – our 'fellow travellers' so to speak – that we mastered the techniques necessary for our quite unaesthetic purpose.

In fact, even on the evidence of Grierson's writings alone, the relationship was not like this. In the 1930s Grierson tried to construct an aesthetic that was consistent with his basic ideology and so avoid any conflict between aesthetic and propagandist aims.

This aesthetic was based on a rejection of Romanticism and a firm distinction between the Public and the Private. Romanticism was associated with the private, the realm of self-expression, personal indulgence, art for art's sake and social irresponsibility. This was an outmoded position. The new aesthetic must be based on a conception of the public. The artist's themes should be social themes not private ones; the artist should express the needs of the State rather than his own needs; art was not his main purpose, it was a by-product of a job well done; the artist should discipline himself by becoming part of a collective body. This aesthetic bound the documentary movement together in the 1930s. A distinction between aesthetes and propagandists was always implicit but only became manifest in the 1940s under the demands made by the war.

The films made in the first phase (up until the mid 1930s) reflect the aesthetic position that Grierson had developed. *Night Mail*, *Coalface*, *Shipyard*, *Aero Engine*, *Industrial Britain* do not immediately provoke the question of whether they were made for aesthetic or propagandist reasons. The split becomes more obvious in the late 1930s when the film-makers began to experiment with different documentary forms. Most important was the development of the lecture film where the film's visuals simply served to illustrate a commentary. (*Housing Problems* and *Children at School* are among the best examples of this tendency.) At the same time there were also a number of aesthetic experiments. The most influential was the development of the dramatic documentary film, which was built around stories drawn from actual happenings but then re-created. The re-creation sometimes involved studio work but the actors were non-professional and usually people who had been involved in the events the story was built around. Harry Watt's *The Saving of Bill Blewett* and *North Sea* are good examples. Apart from this there were various idiosyncratic experiments like Len Lye's abstract films and Cavalcanti's whimsical fable, *Pett and Pott*.

Cavalcanti always had a general influence on the documentary movement because of his prestige, but his influence must have been more precise when he took charge of the GPO film unit in 1937 after Grierson left to work at Film Centre. Throughout his career he had shown an interest in formal experiments. In the late 1920s he had been involved in the French avant-garde film movement. He had produced the first of the symphonic documentaries, *Rien que les Heures*. All his work with the British documentary movement had experimental qualities – sound in *Coalface*, subject and approach in *Pett and Pott*, approach in *Happy in the Morning*. He was the producer of *The Saving of Bill Blewett* and *North Sea*, and also the producer of Humphrey Jennings' early films

(Jennings had taken an active part in the making of *Pett and Pott*).

For obvious reasons, the war weighted the balance in favour of the directly propagandist film. Although some formal experiment continued – the dramatic documentary was developed on a much larger scale with films like *Target for Tonight, Fires were Started* and *Western Approaches* (which was even made in colour) – the British documentary film had a narrower perspective at the end of the war than it had had in the 1930s. The change is reflected in Grierson's writings. His writings during and after the war show a less specific interest in the cinema and not much concern with aesthetic problems. They nearly all centre on discussions of his general social philosophy.

Almost inevitably discussion of the documentary film after the end of the war was dominated by what was felt to be the 'crisis' of documentary. It was thought that films of the quality of those made in the 1930s were no longer being produced. The crisis was put down mainly to the failure of sponsorship, particularly on the part of the Labour Government. Later writers about the period (like Dilys Powell and David Robinson) attributed the failure to the arrival of the Labour Government, which made redundant the social aims that had animated the film-makers in the 1930s. Both these explanations are undoubtedly relevant but they need to be seen in a wider perspective.

The documentary film of the 1930s had exploited a very particular situation where the ideas of intellectuals, potentially social critics, coincided with the interests of some State, and large scale private organisations. This convergence sprang from a common belief in the need for some form of rationalised mass society, within the general framework of modern, post-Keynesian capitalism. Basil Wright described the situation very well:

In a few years you had the purveyors of light and heat providing, in films, in exhibitions and handbooks, discussions of basic national issues – housing, nutrition and education. In so doing they transformed the public's conception of them overnight – and as far as business, well, more houses meant more lighting and heating; more and better food and cooking meant the same. It worked all ways.

The election of a Labour Government in 1945 marked a general public recognition of the need for State intervention in society. This recognition removed any potential critical edge from the intellectuals' position and made the film-makers into direct propagandists for the government. There was also a much more complex bureaucratic system after the war. In the 1930s the people directly responsible for sponsoring the films had no clear idea of what they were doing and this gave the film-makers a good deal of freedom from sponsors' interventions. As sponsors became more familiar with the purposes of this kind of film-making, they began to interfere more directly. This not only led to frustration on the film-makers' part but also narrowed the scope of the films, which became much more directly promotional. The general ideological purpose that Grierson had in mind for the documentary film was lost sight of. These general changes in the situation were compounded by the absence of anybody in the Labour Government with a real enthusiasm for the use of film as an instrument of propaganda. The one man who did have this enthusiasm seems to have been Sir Stafford Cripps, but he was too preoccupied with economic issues to give the documentary film-makers any help.

The pre-war situation also changed in another way. The documentary film-makers of that time had always considered themselves part of the cinema as a whole and had taken an active interest in what was happening throughout the cinema. Magazines like *World Film News* and *Cinema Quarterly*, although taking a special interest in the documentary film, were general film magazines in intention. But as the structure that had been created for the documentary film became self-sufficient it inevitably separated the documentary film from the rest of cinema, making it into a parochial world of its own. This

Basil Wright directing *The Country Comes to Town* (1932)

change was marked by the name and character of the magazine that replaced *World Film News*, *Documentary News Letter*, which only devoted a small part of its attention to the feature film. This isolation of the documentary film also meant that the link with the film societies became a less intimate one. The split between the documentary and the rest of the cinema was finally marked by the emergence of a new generation of critics. In the magazine *Sequence*, quite different attitudes from those of the documentary film-makers were expressed, and in so far as *Sequence* showed any interest in the mainstream British documentary film, it was vaguely hostile.

By the end of the 1940s the documentary had become essentially what it is today: a specialised world having no vital links with the general cinema, constrained by sponsors who thought in strictly utilitarian terms. The attempt made by Grierson and other members of the original documentary group like Paul

33

Harry Watt

Rotha and Basil Wright to solve the situation by extending the
aims of the documentary movement to deal with international
questions like the world food situation, medical problems, etc,
failed mainly because they were not able to create an international structure to support their work and, presumably, because internationalism was not the easiest ideology to propa-
gate in the years of the Cold War. If the documentary film has
been revivified at all in recent years, it has been from new
sources like cinema-*vérité* and television.

The influence of the British documentary film movement

It is difficult to make a definitive critical estimate of the films
produced by the documentary movement. In part, this is
because many of the subjects of the films are outmoded, the
social issues they refer to are no longer relevant. Even those
films which are not simply attempts to call attention to social

issues, which reveal a definite aesthetic impulse, are difficult to discuss critically. They seem remote, abstract. The films that it is possible to make connection with are the work of marginal figures like Humphrey Jennings and Len Lye.

The importance of the documentary movement lies, not in the quality of individual films, but in the impact it had in general on the British cinema. Grierson captured the interest in film as an art that was developing in Britain in the late 1920s for the documentary movement. In effect, this meant that the documentary film became the British art film. So both film-making and critical discussion have been profoundly affected by the documentary conception.

In general terms this can be said to have produced a bias against the commercial, fiction cinema, except where that cinema has adopted documentary modes. Today the effect is not a strong one. Grierson and the documentary film are un-fashionable, dismissed as of little interest by younger film-makers and critics. Yet the ideas that were developed in the late 1930s have never been seriously challenged; the structure of the documentary industry is still the one that Grierson did so much to create. The result is that an important and influential sector of the British cinema is still shackled by a conception of the cinema developed by Grierson and his associates (many of whom are still active, particularly as producers).

The best tribute that the British cinema could now pay these pioneers is to acknowledge their importance by challenging their ideas and influence. A new conception of the cinema, a different film-making structure – the task is an enormous one. But unless it is taken up, the British cinema seems likely to continue to drift, a prisoner of the past, with no clear notion of its future.

Filmography: Grierson as producer and director

The filmography which follows does not claim to be a complete record of all British documentary films 1929–1962, but lists those films in which Grierson himself had a close and direct influence.

John Grierson

1898	Born in Deanstown, Perthshire.
1923	Graduated from Glasgow University. Travelled in the United States on a Rockefeller Fellowship for three years. Associated with the Department of Political Science, University of Chicago.
1927	Joined the Empire Marketing Board Film Unit, under Sir Stephen Tallents, for research into government use of mass media.
1928	Film Officer. Produced *Drifters* and then *Song of Ceylon*.
1933	Became head of the GPO Film Unit when the Empire Marketing Board was dissolved and the Film Unit transferred to the GPO, and produced a number of documentary films including *Night Mail*.
1937	Resigned to form the Film Centre (of which he remained a director), with Arthur Elton, Stuart Legg and J. P. R. Golightly.
1937–40	Film Adviser to the Imperial Relations Trust, and to the Canadian, Australian and New Zealand Governments.
1939–45	Film Commissioner for Canada, guiding legislation leading to the establishment of the National Film Board of Canada, and, with Stuart Legg, producing the series *The World in Action*. This included *Churchill's Island* (Oscar 1941).
1947	Co-ordinator of Mass Media at UNESCO.
1948	Controller, Films Division of the Central Office of Information.
1951–54	Joint Executive Producer of Group Three (an experimental group established by the National Film Finance Company). Produced, among others, *The Brave Don't Cry* and *Laxdale Hall*.

1954   Resigned from the Central Office of Information. A member of the Films of Scotland Committee. Wrote the treatment for *Seawards the Great Ships* (Oscar 1961).

1955   Produced and presented the television series *This Wonderful World* for Scottish TV, which ran for ten years.

Grierson wrote and spoke extensively on films, including lectures in Canada in 1969. *Grierson on Documentary*, a collection of his writings edited by H. Forsyth Hardy, was first published in 1946, and revised in 1966 (Faber & Faber).

Honorary Doctorate of Laws (1948); Hon. D.Litt. (1969); Commander of the British Empire (1961); and holder of the Golden Thistle Award (Edinburgh Festival 1968). He died in February 1972.

Grierson as Director

Drifters (1929)

Production company   New Era Films for the Empire Marketing Board
Producer/Director/Script John Grierson
Photography   Basil Emmott

Shown in Film Society Programme 33, 10 November 1929
Running time: 50 min
Distributor: Central Film Library

Grierson as Producer
Conquest (1930) (An experimental compilation film, drawn from a number of U.S. films)

Production company   Empire Marketing Board Film Unit
Constructed by   John Grierson, assisted by Basil Wright

Shown in Film Society Programme 42, 16 November 1930
Running time: 31 min
Copy held in National Film Archive

The Country Comes to Town (1931)

Production company	Empire Marketing Board Film Unit
Producer	John Grierson
Director	Basil Wright
Photography	James Burger, Basil Wright

Running time: 18 min
Copy held in National Film Archive

Shadow on the Mountain (1931)

Production company	Empire Marketing Board Film Unit
Producer	John Grierson
Director	Arthur Elton
Photography	Jack Miller

Running time: 15 min
Copy held in National Film Archive

Upstream (1931)

Production company	Empire Marketing Board Film Unit
Producer	John Grierson
Director	Arthur Elton
Photography	Jack Miller
Commentary spoken by	Andrew Buchanan

Running time: 18 min
Print not available in G.B.

Industrial Britain (1931–2)

Production company   Empire Marketing Board Film Unit
Producer/Editor   John Grierson with Edgar Anstey
Director/Photography   Robert Flaherty

Running time: 22 min
Distributor: British Film Institute

King Log (1932) (originally *Lumber*, with a new soundtrack)

Production company   Empire Marketing Board Film Unit
Producer   John Grierson
Director/Editor   Basil Wright

Running time: 19 min
Copy held in National Film Archive

The New Generation (1932)

Production company   New Era Films
Producer   John Grierson
Director/Editor   Stuart Legg
Photography   Gerald Gibbs

Shown in Film Society Programme 61, 12 February 1933
Running time: 25 min
Print not available in G.B.

The New Operator (1932)

Production company   Empire Marketing Board Film Unit for GPO
Producer   John Grierson

| Director | Stuart Legg |
| Photography | Gerald Gibbs |

Running time: 10 min
Copy held in National Film Archive

O'er Hill and Dale (1932)

Production company	Empire Marketing Board Film Unit
Producer	John Grierson
Director/Photography	Basil Wright
Commentary spoken by	Andrew Buchanan

Running time: 17 min
Copy held in National Film Archive

The Voice of the World (1932)

Production company	New Era Films for the Gramophone Company, London
Producer	John Grierson
Director	Arthur Elton
Photography	George Noble

Shown in Film Society Programme 63, 2 April 1933
Running time: 30 min (approx)
Print not available in G.B.

Aero-Engine (1933)

Production company	Empire Marketing Board Film Unit
Producer	John Grierson
Director/Script	Arthur Elton

| Photography | George Noble |
| Editor | Arthur Elton |

Running time: 55 min
Copy held in National Film Archive

Cargo From Jamaica (1933)

Production company	Empire Marketing Board Film Unit
Producer	John Grierson
Director/Photography	Basil Wright

Running time: 11 min
Copy held in National Film Archive

The Coming of the Dial (1933)

Production company	GPO Film Unit
Producer	John Grierson
Director	Stuart Legg
Photography	Gerald Gibbs

Running time: 15 min
Copy held in National Film Archive

Eskimo Village (1933)

Production company	Empire Marketing Board Film Unit for the Admiralty
Producer	John Grierson
Director	Edgar Anstey

Liner Cruising South (1933)

Production company	Empire Marketing Board Film Unit for Orient Line
Producer	John Grierson
Director/Photography	Basil Wright

Running time: 44 min
Copy held in National Film Archive

So This Is London (1933)

Production company	Empire Marketing Board Film Unit for Strand Film Co. for the Travel Association
Producer	John Grierson
Director	Marion Grierson
Photography	W. Shenton
Music	J. Foulds

Running time: 20 min
Copy held in National Film Archive (National Film Theatre)

Telephone Workers (1933)

Production company	GPO Film Unit
Producer	John Grierson
Director	Stuart Legg
Photography	Gerald Gibbs

Running time: 25 min
Copy held in National Film Archive

Uncharted Waters (1933)

Production company	Empire Marketing Board Film Unit for the Admiralty
Producer	John Grierson
Director/Photography/ Editor	Edgar Anstey

Windmill in Barbados (1933)

Production company	Empire Marketing Board Film Unit
Producer	John Grierson
Director/Photography	Basil Wright
Sound Supervision	Cavalcanti
Sound	E. A. Pawley

Running time: 9 min (approx)
Copy held in National Film Archive

BBC: Droitwich (1934)

Production company	GPO Film Unit for the BBC
Producer	John Grierson
Directors	Edgar Anstey, Harry Watt
Photography	Edgar Anstey
Commentary	A. S. Hibberd
Sound	E. A. Pawley

Running time: 16 min
Copy held in National Film Archive

Granton Trawler (1934)

Production company	Empire Marketing Board Film Unit
Producer/Photography	John Grierson
Editor	Edgar Anstey

Running time: 11 min
Copy held in National Film Archive

Pett and Pott (1934)

Production company	GPO Film Unit
Producer	John Grierson
Director	Cavalcanti
Assistant directors	Basil Wright, Stuart Legg
Photography	John Taylor
Sets	Humphrey Jennings
Music	Walter Leigh
Sound recording	John Cox

Good citizens: J. M. Reeves (*Mr Pett*), Marjorie Fone (*Mrs Pett*), June
   Godfrey (*Polly Pett*), Bruce Winston (*Judge*)
Evil citizens: Eric Hudson (*Mr Pott*), Barbara Nixon (*Mrs Pott*), Jack Scott
   (*Burglar*), Valeska Girt (*Maid*)
Running time: 33 min
Distributor: British Film Institute

Post Haste (1934)

Production company	GPO Film Unit
Producer	John Grierson
Editor	Humphrey Jennings

Running time: 33 min
Copy held in National Film Archive

44

Six-Thirty Collection (1934)

Production company	GPO Film Unit
Producer	John Grierson
Directors	Edgar Anstey, Harry Watt
Photography	J. D. Davidson
Sound recording	J. Cox

Running time: 16 min
Copy held in National Film Archive

Song of Ceylon (1934)

Production company	GPO Film Unit for Ceylon Tea Marketing Board
Producer	John Grierson
Director/Editor/ Photography	Basil Wright
Assistant director	John Taylor
Script	John Grierson, Basil Wright and others, partly from a book on Ceylon written by the traveller Robert Knox in 1680
Commentary spoken by	Lionel Wendt
Music	Composed by and recorded under the direction of Walter Leigh
Sound supervision	Cavalcanti
Sound recording	E. A. Pawley

Running time: 40 min
Distributors: British Film Institute/Central Film Library

Spring Comes to England (1934)

Production company	Empire Marketing Board Film Unit for the Ministry of Agriculture
Producer	John Grierson with A. V. Campbell

Basil Wright during the shooting of *Song of Ceylon* (above); and Edgar Anstey
(1932)

46

Director	Donald Taylor
Photography	F. H. Jones
Music	J. Foulds

Running time: 12 min
Copy held in National Film Archive

Spring on the Farm (1934)

Production company	New Era/Empire Marketing Board Film Unit
Producer	John Grierson
Director	Evelyn Spice
Photography	A. E. Jeakins

Running time: 9 min
Copy held in National Film Archive

Weather Forecast (1934)

Production company	GPO Film Unit
Producer	John Grierson
Director	Evelyn Spice
Photography	George Noble
Sound Supervision	Cavalcanti

Running time: 20 min
Copy held in National Film Archive

BBC: The Voice of Britain (1935)

Production company	GPO Film Unit for the BBC (with the co-operation of BBC engineers)
Producers	John Grierson, Stuart Legg
Director/Script/Editor	Stuart Legg and others
Photography	George Noble, J. D. Davidson, W. Shenton

Music	Played by Adrian Boult and the BBC Symphony Orchestra; Henry Hall and the BBC Dance Orchestra
Sound recording	E. A. Pawley

Running time: 56 min
Copy held in National Film Archive

Coalface (1935)

Production company	GPO Film Unit
Producer	John Grierson
Director/Script	Cavalcanti
Verse	W. H. Auden, Montagu Slater
Editor	William Coldstream
Music	Benjamin Britten
Sound supervision	Cavalcanti, Stuart Legg, Benjamin Britten
Sound recording	E. A. Pawley

Running time: 10 min
Distributor: British Film Institute

Introducing the Dial (1935)

Production company	GPO Film Unit
Producer	John Grierson
Director	Stuart Legg
Photography	Gerald Gibbs

Running time: 6 min
Copy held in National Film Archive

Night Mail (1936)

Production company	GPO Film Unit
Producer	John Grierson

Directors	Harry Watt, Basil Wright
Script	John Grierson, Basil Wright, Harry Watt
Verse	W. H. Auden
Photography	Henry Fowle, Jonah Jones
Editors	Basil Wright, R. Q. McNaughton
Music	Benjamin Britten
Sound supervision	Cavalcanti
Sound recording	A. E. Pawley

Running time: 25 min
Distributor: Central Film Library

The Saving of Bill Blewett (1936)

Production company	GPO Film Unit
Producer	John Grierson
Associate producer	Cavalcanti
Director/Script	Harry Watt
Photography	S. Onions, Jonah Jones
Music	Benjamin Britten

Running time: 25 min
Distributor: British Film Institute

Trade Tattoo (1936)

Production company	GPO Film Unit
Producer	John Grierson
Director	Len Lye
Music Editor	Jack Ellitt
Music	Played by the Lecuona Band

Running time: 5 min
Distributor: British Film Institute

Calendar of the Year (1937)

Production company	GPO Film Unit
Producer	John Grierson
Director	Evelyn Spice
Photography	Jonah Jones, Henry Fowle
Music	Benjamin Britten
Sound recording	E. K. Webster

Running time: 17 min
Copy held in National Film Archive

Children at School (1937)

Production company	Realist Film Unit for British Commercial Gas Association
Producers	John Grierson, Basil Wright
Director	Basil Wright
Commentary	H. Wilson Harris
Photography	A. E. Jeakins

Running time: 20 min
Distributor: British Film Institute (restricted use)

Four Barriers (1937)

Production company	GPO Film Unit with Pro Telephon, Zurich
Producers	John Grierson, Harry Watt
Director	Cavalcanti
Photography	John Taylor

Running time: 8 min
Print not available in G.B.

Job in a Million (1937)

Production company	GPO Film Unit in co-operation with London Postal Region
Producer	John Grierson
Director	Evelyn Spice
Editor	Norman McLaren
Photography	S. Onions
Music	Brian Easdale
Sound recording	G. C. Diamond

Running time: 41 min
Copy held in National Film Archive

Line to Tschierva Hut (1937)

Production company	GPO Film Unit and Pro Telephon, Zurich
Producer	John Grierson
Director	Cavalcanti
Photography	John Taylor
Music	Maurice Jaubert

Running time: 10 min
Copy held in National Film Archive

The Smoke Menace (1937)

Production company	Realist Film Unit for the British Commercial Gas Association
Producers	John Grierson, Basil Wright
Director	John Taylor
Commentary	Professor J. B. S. Haldane

Running time: 14 min
Copy held in National Film Archive

We Live in Two Worlds (1937)

Production company	GPO Film Unit and Pro Telephon, Zurich
Producer	John Grierson
Director	Cavalcanti
Narration and script	J. B. Priestley
Photography	John Taylor
Editor	R. Q. McNaughton
Music	Maurice Jaubert
Sound recording	E. K. Webster

Running time: 15 min
Copy held in National Film Archive

The Face of Scotland (1938)

Production company	Realist Film Unit for Films of Scotland Committee
Producer	John Grierson
Director	Basil Wright
Photography	A. E. Jeakins
Music	Walter Leigh
Sound recording	W. F. Elliott

Running time: 20 min
Copy held in National Film Archive

The Londoners (1939)

Production company	Realist Film Unit for the British Commercial Gas Association
Producers	John Grierson, Basil Wright
Director	John Taylor (assisted by Philip Leacock)
Script	John Taylor
Verse	W. H. Auden
Photography	A. E. Jeakins
Editor	Alan Gourlay

Commentary spoken by   Howard Marshall
Sound recording   H. G. Halstead

Running time: 24 min
Copy held in National Film Archive

Man of Africa (1953)

Production company	Group Three
Producer	John Grierson
Director	Cyril Frankel
Script	Montagu Slater
Commentary	Gordon Heath
Photography	Denny Densham
Colour process	Ferraniacolour
Editor	Alvin Bailey
Music	Malcolm Arnold
Sound	John Mitchell

Frederick Bijurenda (*Jonathan*), Violet Mukabureza (*Violet*), Mattayo
Bukwira ('*Soldier*')
Running time: 44 min
Distributor: Regent

Grierson as Executive Producer (mainly features)

Group Three Productions
1951   *Judgment Deferred, Brandy for the Parson*
1952   *The Brave Don't Cry, Laxdale Hall, The Oracle, Time Gentlemen
       Please, You're Only Young Twice*
1953   *Man of Africa* (documentary produced by Grierson)
1954   *Orders Are Orders*

Grierson was especially interested in the production of *The Brave Don't
Cry*, and was greatly involved in the making of the film.

The Brave Don't Cry (1952)

Production company	Group Three
Executive producer	John Grierson
Associate producer	Isobel Pargiter
Production controller	John Baxter
Director	Philip Leacock
Assistant director	Denis Johnson
Original screenplay	Montagu Slater
Additional dialogue	Lindsay Galloway
Photography	Arthur Grant
Camera operator	Ken Hodges
Editor	John Trumper
Art Director	Michael Stringer
Sound recordist	Len Page

John Gregson (*John Cameron*), Meg Buchanan (*Margaret Wishart*), John Rae (*Donald Sloan*), Fulton MacKay (*Dan Wishart*), Andrew Keir (*Charlie Ross*), Wendy Noel (*Jean Knox*), Russell Waters (*Hughie Aitken*), Jameson Clark (*Dr. Andrew Keir*), Eric Woodburn (*Rab Elliott*), Archie Duncan (*Walter Hardie*), Jack Stewart (*Willie Duncan*), Anne Butchart (*Biddy Ross*), Mac Picton (*Jin Knox*), Jock McKay (*Jock Woods*), Jean Anderson (*Mrs. Sloan*), John Singer (*Tam Stewart*), Chris Page (*George*), Kelty Macleod (*Mrs. Duncan*), Hal Osmond (*Sandy Mackenzie*), Guthrie Mason (*Jamie Knox*), Howard Connell (*Hughie's messenger*), Russell Hunter (*Police Sergeant*), Sam Kydd (*Porter*)
Running time: 90 min
Distributor: ABFD
Produced at Southall Studios, and on location in Scotland
Selected to open the Sixth Edinburgh Film Festival, 1952

Films Based on Treatments by Grierson

Seawards the Great Ships (1959)

Production company	Templar Film Studios for the Films of Scotland Committee
Director	Hilary Harris, from an outline treatment by John Grierson
Commentary	Clifford Hanley

Commentary spoken by	Bryden Murdoch
Photography	Hilary Harris
Animation	James Macaulay
Colour process	Eastman
Editor	Hilary Harris

Running time: 29 min
Distribution (theatrical): Rank; (non-theatrical): Central Office of Information

Heart of Scotland (1961–2)

Production company	Templar Film Studios for the Films of Scotland Committee
Producer	A. Riddell Black
Director	Lawrence Henson, from a treatment by John Grierson
Photography	Edward McConnell
Colour Process	Eastman
Music	Frank Spedding
Sound	John Ormond
Narrator	Bryden Murdoch

Running time: 25 min
Distribution (theatrical): MGM; (non-theatrical): Central Film Library

Biographical Notes: Grierson's associates

Edgar Anstey

Born at Watford in 1907. Left the Department of Scientific and Industrial Research to join John Grierson at the Empire Marketing Board Film Unit in 1930 where he directed *Uncharted Waters, Eskimo Village* (1933), and *Granton Trawler* (1934); then *Six-Thirty Collection* (1934) with Harry Watt, for the GPO Film Unit. In 1934–5 he organised the Shell Film Unit, and directed several documentaries for the British Commercial Gas Association – *Dinner Hour* and *Housing Problems* (1935) with Arthur Elton, and *Enough to Eat* (1936). He was also Director of Productions for March of Time till 1938, and spent some time as Foreign Editor in New York. In 1940 he joined the Board of Directors at the Film Centre, and acted through the Centre as producer in charge of the Shell Film Unit, and as consultant to documentary film sponsors. During the war he produced many documentaries for the MOI and others, and was afterwards a radio broadcaster and film critic, as a member of the Films Council and through the Film Centre. As Films Officer for the British Transport Commission he organised and supervised British Transport Films, including *Journey Into Spring* (1957), *Between the Tides* (1958) and *Terminus* (1961). In 1956 he was appointed Chairman of the British Film Academy, and in 1961 President of the International Scientific Film Association.

Alberto Cavalcanti

Born in 1897 in Rio De Janeiro, Brazil, educated at Geneva Fine Art School, he qualified as an architect, and began his film career as art director.

57

In Paris he produced and directed a number of films including *Rien que les Heures* (1926) and *En Rade* (1928). In 1934 he joined Grierson at the GPO Film Unit, later the Crown Film Unit, and edited, produced and directed numerous documentaries. As a director, his best-known films are: *Pett and Pott* and *Glorious Sixth of June* (1934); *Coalface* (1935) and *Message from Geneva* (1936); *Line to Tschierva Hut, Who Writes to Switzerland?* and *We Live In Two Worlds* (1937); *Cause Commune* (1938), and a sequence of *Mony a Pickle* (1938). In 1940 he joined Ealing Studios as director and associate producer, where he made the feature-length documentary *Yellow Caesar* (1941), and the features *Went the Day Well* (1943), *Champagne Charlie* (1944), and co-directed *Dead of Night* (1945). After leaving Ealing he made *Nicholas Nickleby* (1947), *They Made Me a Fugitive* (1947), *For Them that Trespass* (1948) and *The First Gentleman* (1949). In 1950 he returned to Brazil to produce a series of documentary films, and since then has worked on features in Europe and lectured in America. His collected essays have been published under the title *Film and Reality*.

Sir Arthur Elton

Born in 1906, educated at Marlborough and Cambridge, he joined the scenario department at Gainsborough in 1927, also working as copywriter and scriptwriter before joining the Empire Marketing Board Film Unit under Grierson in 1929, where he directed *Shadow on the Mountain* and *Upstream* (1931); *The Voice of the World* (1932) for H.M.V.; and *Aero-Engine* (1933). In 1934 he became documentary film producer for the Ministry of Labour, and directed *Workers and Jobs* (1935); also a number of films for the British Commercial Gas Association, including *Housing Problems* (1935) with Edgar Anstey, and *Men Behind the Meters* (1935). In 1936 he succeeded Edgar Anstey as producer in charge of the Shell Film Unit, and produced a large number of films, including *Transfer of Power*. Together with John Grierson and Basil Wright he founded Film Centre in 1937. Early in 1941 he was made Supervisor of Film Production in the Films Division of the Ministry of Information under Jack Beddington, and in 1944 was elected Chairman of the Scientific Film Association. In 1946 he was appointed Film Adviser to the Danish Government, and in 1947 nominated by the Foreign Office as Film Adviser to the Control Commission of Germany. He returned to Britain in 1948 and took up his post of Film Adviser to Shell. He was a Governor of the British Film Institute 1948–9, in 1951 joint author of *Film Production in Six Countries* for UNESCO, and Head of Central Films for Shell 1957–60. He is now Chairman of Film Centre International.

Stuart Legg

Born in London in 1907, attended Marlborough College, and St John's College, Cambridge. He began as director and editor with British Instructional Films in 1931, then worked with the Empire Marketing Board Film Unit and the GPO Film Unit until 1937. During that time he directed *The New Generation* and *The New Operator* (1932); *Telephone Workers* (1932–3); *Cable Ship* and *The Coming of the Dial* (1933); *Conquering Space* and *BBC: The Voice of Britain* (1935); and co-directed *Roadways* (1937). He was then at Film Centre, where he was at one time Business Manager of World Film News, and wrote the controversial book *Money Behind the Screen*. He was Director of Production for Strand Film Company in 1937. Later he worked with John Grierson as chief producer to the National Film Board of Canada, being associated especially during the war with the *World in Action* series. After working in New York, he joined the Crown Film Unit in England, and from there in 1950 went to Film Centre International, where he was involved in films on international themes for Shell and others (including *The Rival World* and *Song of the Clouds*). Since that time he has acted as guest producer to the Commonwealth Film Unit in Australia, and is a director of Film Centre International. At present he is writing at his home in Wiltshire.

Paul Rotha

Born in London in 1907, studied at the Slade School, and was a painter, designer and art critic before joining the Empire Marketing Board Film Unit. In the thirties he directed a number of documentary films for industrial sponsors, including *Contact* (1933) for Shell-Mex and B.P.; and for Gaumont British Instructional Films, *Rising Tide* (1934) sponsored by the Southern Railway; *Shipyard* (1935) sponsored by Orient Shipping Line and Vickers Armstrong, and *The Face of Britain* (1935). He was also Director of Production for Strand Film Company (1936–8), produced films for the Realist Film Unit, and directed *The Fourth Estate* (1939–40) for *The Times*. Paul Rotha Productions was formed in 1941: as managing director

59

he produced numerous films for the company and directed *World of Plenty* (1943) for the Ministry of Information. For Films of Fact (a later division of Paul Rotha Productions) he produced and directed *Total War in Britain* (1945), *Land of Promise* (1946), and *The World is Rich* (1947), all for the Central Office of Information; and *A City Speaks* (1947) for Manchester City Corporation. In 1950 he went into feature films and directed *No Resting Place* (a blend of documentary and fiction) for Colin Lesslie Productions. Then in 1953 he co-directed with Basil Wright *World Without End* for UNESCO, and moved to head the BBC Television Documentary Unit. In 1957 he wrote, produced and directed the feature *Cat and Mouse* for Anvil Films, and was Chairman of the British Film Academy. He made a film on the Abbey Theatre in 1959, *Cradle of Genius*, and since then has directed features in Germany and Holland – *Life of Adolf Hitler* (1961) and *The Silent Raid* (1962). He has written extensively on the cinema: his books include *The Film Till Now, Celluloid, Movie Parade, The Film Today, Documentary Film* and *Rotha on the Film*. At present he is writing an autobiographical account of the British documentary movement.

Harry Watt

Born in Edinburgh, 1906, studied at Edinburgh University, and joined the Empire Marketing Board Film Unit in 1931. With the GPO Film Unit he wrote and directed documentary films, including a series of March of Time subjects. Among his films are *Six-Thirty Collection* (1934) with Edgar Anstey, *BBC Droitwich* (1934), *Night Mail* (1936) with Basil Wright, *The Saving of Bill Blewett, Men of the Alps*, and *Sorting Office* (1936); *Four Barriers* (1937); *Big Money, North Sea* and *Health in Industry* (1938); *The First Days* (1939) with Jennings and Jackson; *Britain at Bay, London Can Take It* with Jennings, *Squadron 992* and *Dover – Front Line* (1940). From the outbreak of war he worked with the Ministry of Information on propaganda films, as associate producer of the Crown Film Unit, and for the Army Film Unit. Documentaries he directed during this time include *The Story of an Air Communiqué* (1940), *Christmas Under Fire* and *Target for Tonight* (1941), and *Twenty-One Miles* (1942). He joined Ealing Studios in 1942 and directed and wrote the screenplay for them for the documentary-style feature *Nine Men*, followed by the feature *Fiddlers Three* (1944) and the screenplay for *For Those In Peril* (1944). In Australia from 1945 to 1948 he directed two more features, *The Overlanders* (1945–6) and *Eureka Stockade* (1946–8), and then in Africa he wrote and directed *Where No Vultures Fly* (1951), and directed *West of Zanzibar* (1953). He joined

Granada TV as a producer in 1955, and resigned the following year to join Ealing again as a director, where he wrote and directed *The Siege of Pinchgut* (1959). He has again worked for Granada, and has made a documentary for UNESCO – *People Like Maria* (1958).

Basil Wright

Born in London, 1907, educated at Sherborne and Corpus Christi, Cambridge. From 1929 onwards he was associated with John Grierson, first as an assistant, and then as producer and director, at the Empire Marketing Board Film Unit and GPO Film Unit, where he directed *The Country Comes to Town* (1931); *O'er Hill and Dale* and *King Log* (1932); *Cargo from Jamaica, Liner Cruising South,* and *Windmill In Barbados* (1933); *Song of Ceylon* (1934); and *Night Mail* with Harry Watt (1936). In 1937 he formed the Realist Film Unit, directing *Children at School* (1937), *The Face of Scotland* (1938), and *Filling the Gap* (1942). In the forties he was at the Film Centre, producing documentaries for the Ministry of Information, and wrote film criticism for *The Spectator*, then worked as producer in charge of the Crown Film Unit (1945), where he made *This Was Japan, Unrelenting Struggle* and *Southern Rhodesia* (1945). During the war he spent some time in Canada as adviser on information technique and policy, and immediately afterwards worked at UNESCO under Sir Julian Huxley and John Grierson. In 1946 he founded International Realist, and produced documentaries up to 1949, directing *Bernard Miles on Gundogs* in 1948. Since then he has directed *Waters of Time* (1951) for the Port of London Authority's contribution to the Festival of Britain, and co-directed with Paul Rotha *World Without End* (1953); also in 1954 produced a film *The Drawings of Leonardo da Vinci*, and directed *Stained Glass at Fairford* (1956) for the Arts Council. His award-winning films on Greece, *The Immortal Land* (1958) and *Greek Sculpture*, were followed by a film for the Worshipful Company of Goldsmiths, *A Place for Gold* (1960). He has also lectured, and written a book, *Use of the Film*.

2: Humphrey Jennings

He was, he remains, one of those few people who feel that in this threatened world we have no longer much time, we have no longer all eternity before us, and if we wish to communicate with people we must do it quickly – Nicole Védrès

Jennings' intellectual background

'Individual vision' (Grierson), 'genius' (Basil Wright), 'startling originality' (Gavin Lambert), 'unique and irreplaceable' (Ian Dalrymple), 'the only real poet the British cinema has yet produced' (Lindsay Anderson). These are the phrases one meets in critical accounts of the work of Humphrey Jennings, the British cinema's one undoubted *auteur*, though his reputation rests on a handful of short films and only one feature-length work, all documentaries, most of them made during the Second World War. Jennings has often been regarded as a product, and probably the culminating talent, of the British documentary movement of the 1930s. Yet Jennings himself remained rather aloof from the movement and made his first personal film only in 1939, after Grierson's departure. The documentary movement gave Jennings a tradition, a context in which to work, but there can be little doubt that what makes his films exceptional derives primarily from the particular background of culture and ideas he brought to the cinema.

Jennings was quite unashamedly an intellectual and an artist, and when he began working in the popular medium of the cinema he brought with him his artistic and intellectual concerns, doing so, as Nicole Védrès says, 'without any concession, without any surrender of taste.' Jennings' intellectual formation informs his films to such an extent that any understanding of them must begin by some explanation of his background, fully and interestingly described by friends and critics like Kathleen Raine, Jacob Bronowski, Charles Madge, Gerald Noxon, James Merralls.

A Suffolk-born Englishman, educated at Cambridge (the Perse School and Pembroke College), Jennings was from an early age steeped in English culture – Shakespeare, Marlowe, Milton, Blake, Constable forming for him 'a permanent frame of reference'. At university, Jennings specialised in Elizabethan drama and poetry and, as a post-graduate in the early 30s, worked on Shakespeare and Gray, but he was also involved with the science-orientated literary group which produced the magazine *Experiment*. The magazine's editors and contributors included Empson, mathematician, poet and critic, Kathleen Raine, physicist, poet and critic, Bronowski, mathematician and critic, and also Malcolm Lowry, Julian Trevelyan, Basil Wright, Richard Eberhart (as well as outside contributors like Joyce, Mayakovsky, Eluard, Pasternak). Newton, Faraday, Darwin and others were read 'for their poetic content, that is their intellectual vigour, as much as for their science.'

Jennings' complementary interest in literature and science, together with the left-wing views current in the intellectual milieu of the time, led him to a lifelong fascination with the Industrial Revolution, which he saw as a complex inter-relationship of science, industry, social structures and literature. Right up to his death in 1950 Jennings was working on a massive collection of extracts from eighteenth- and nineteenth-century writers, scientists, diarists and so on, chosen to illustrate the transformation in our way of looking at the world between 1660 and 1886. More particularly the book, which was to be called *Pandemonium*, was designed to show the relationship of scientific and social changes to literature. *Pandemonium* was never completed but an early note by Jennings read:

The first stage (1660–1730) is the phase of pure science, direct experiments and clear philosophical and materialist thinking. The invention was as yet only on paper. The people – the impact on life – and consequent exploitation, had not yet arrived. Suggestion: when these ideas, scientific and mechanical, began to be exploited by capital and to involve many human beings, was not this the period of the repression of the clear imaginative vision in ordinary folk? and hence of its being possible for them to be emotionally exploited, e.g. by Wesley?

Charles Madge, who shared Jennings' concerns to a large extent and did some work on the unfinished book after Jennings' death, makes some illuminating comments on this note:

It may help to explain the significance for him of Sir Christopher Wren and St Paul's Cathedral. For him this building, with its rational proportions and forms, was a symbol of what he called 'the first stage'. In the second stage he thought the inhuman, mechanistic side of scientific rationality came uppermost. The building which symbolized this stage was Bentham's Panoptikon, a design for a gaol in which every prisoner would be visible from a central point of observation. In the nineteenth century he thought there was a return to a more human and emotional attitude to life, although the social evils of industrialization were then at their height. The confused optimism of the Great Exhibtion of 1851, and the Crystal Palace in which it was housed, was his symbol for this stage.

Jennings did not see the Industrial Revolution (or for that matter, the whole of English culture) as a thing of the past. He was always aware of the interdependence of past and present. To Jennings, England is both a product and an expression of the past, with its potential for good and evil, beauty and ugliness. This conviction, especially as it concerned the Industrial Revolution, led to his involvement in the late 1930s with Mass Observation, whose aim has been described as

... investigating public opinion qualitatively and quantitatively by the direct observation of behaviour in public places and above all by listening to people's conversations ... a form of loosely organised visual and aural eavesdropping.

Mass Observation was conceived and directed by the anthropologist Tom Harrison and by Charles Madge, who was a Communist. Jennings' political views were certainly left-wing, but he was never politically committed as a Communist. He was attracted by the imaginative materialism of Marxism but felt, for example, that Blake's *Song of Los* said all there was to be said about owners and men in the context of the Industrial Revolution and 'says it much better than Marx did'.

Strangely enough Jennings' interest in Mass Observation may also have stemmed in part from his interest in Surrealism, since both related to his concern for the collective imagination and its expression. He was a close friend of many of the French Surealists. Eluard and Breton had paintings by Jennings in their collections and Eluard wrote a poem about him. He was not only active in staging the 1936 London Surrealist exhibition but also showed some paintings and collages in it. Yet in his ideas on imagery Jennings was independent. In 1931 he was saying that the Surrealists were exploiting 'the rather temporary emotive qualities of incongruity provided by the juxtaposition of objects as objects (with literary associations)'. He called for 'the use of technique as technique, to create mutations in the subject, and the subject thereby to be in its proper place, as the basis of a metamorphosis by paint and not by literary substitution', that is 'to create mutations in the subject' and liberate human perceptions from the literary associations surrounding them.

Jennings also stressed the importance of the public image as against the Surrealists' private images. He disliked the purely personal element in artistic expression. Just as in his poetry he preferred phrases from existing sources, so in painting he always worked from postcards or prints, never from nature. This is equally evident in his films, where he makes

From the Tarot pack

extensive use of popular song, familiar buildings, well-known literature, radio broadcasts and so on. On the whole, Jennings liked his images, as Merralls says, 'particularised, concrete and historical, never invented'. Certain images or subjects return again and again in Jennings' work – St Paul's Cathedral, around which many passages in *Pandemonium* were to centre, the horse and the locomotive (both derived, Kathleen Raine tells us, from the Tarot pack's Chariot, the symbol for human power and achievement),

'Where the black plumes of the horses recede ...' (*Words for Battle*)

the plough, the harvest field, the factory, the industrial landscape.

Jennings' ideas as they related to poetry are interestingly illuminated by one of his war poems:

> I see London
> I see the Dome of Saint Paul's
> like the forehead of Darwin
> I see London stretched away North and North-East
> along dockside roads and balloon-haunted allotments
> Where the black plumes of the horses recede
> and the white helmets of the rescue-squad follow ...
> I see the green leaves of Lincolnshire
> carried through London
> on the wrecked body of an aircraft ...

The poem is almost an illustration of his ideas on poetry: the use of an already existing phrase (the opening, from Blake), the working from particular, concretised and intensely visual images (many of which recur in his films); the derivation of power from the use of actually incongruous juxtaposed images. Perhaps most interesting is the use of allusion in 'the Dome of Saint Paul's / like the forehead of Darwin'. Had the poem spoken of Newton's forehead, it would have encapsulated the image in time, made it specific to an era. But the introduction of Darwin creates an image which spans time and stands for enlightenment in all time.

One of the problems in coming to terms with Jennings – and the problem is most acute in the films – is that although he used public images, these images had associations and connotations which were not usually accessible to the public at large. Most people would not consciously associate the locomotive with the Tarot pack, the horse, the Industrial Revolution. Yet there can be no doubt that when Jennings uses such an image it has, for him, this intense complexity. The best example is St Paul's, a complex symbol for Jennings but perhaps a conventional one for most other people. A shot of St Paul's towering above a mass of rubble is on one level a very simple symbolic image, but Jennings would also have been aware that this particular view of the cathedral revealed vistas that had not been seen for over a century. This kind of gulf between private associations and public perception helps to explain differences of attitude to Jennings – regarded as brilliant by his friends but almost certainly as pretty ordinary by the general public.

Some of Jennings' ideas on art and history would seem to point to the documentary cinema as a likely medium for him but despite frequent contacts with the documentary movement, it was only in 1939 that he began to commit himself to making films.

At Cambridge Jennings was one of the first members of the Film Guild, which showed French, German and Russian films, but his interest was theoretical and critical and he did not join friends like Stuart Legg in trying practical film work. In the early 1930s, Jennings' main interest was painting, but he maintained close contact with Cambridge friends like Legg, Wright and Elton, who were working for the Empire Marketing Board, and from 1933 the General Post Office, under Grierson. Jennings' first film work was in 1934 when Gerald Noxon offered him the chance of making a short advertising film for an American oil company, with the sole aim of relieving his financial problems. Jennings proceeded with enthusiasm to give a forceful physical imagery to a mythical substance called SLUM, to 'produce a direct emotional response from the audience'.

After that he worked on several GPO films, though without becoming a member of the unit. He edited a short film, *Post-Haste* (1934), which described the history of the GPO through old English prints and seems to have been one of the earliest examples of a film composed of still pictures. The angle of vision in prints of a railway viaduct or a train passing under a bridge is reminiscent of similar scenes in later Jennings films and more generally seems to indicate an immersion in an English tradition of imagery. As set designer on the whimsical experimental GPO film *Pett and Pott* (1934), he was apparently responsible for the only interesting moments in the film – those with surreal overtones, like the long facing rows of commuting gentlemen, all dozing off to sleep. Also in 1934, Jennings made *The Story of the Wheel*, a documentary on the evolution of wheeled transport from primitive times to the present. *Locomotives* (1935) expanded on this: using models from the Science Museum, the film shows how steam is made, then traces the use of the steam pump in mills and collieries through to the development of the first locomotives and the spread of the railway network.

With Len Lye, Jennings was involved in making *The Birth of the Robot* (1936), as an experiment with the Gasparcolour colour film process.

Essentially, though, Jennings stayed well clear of the mainstream of Grierson documentaries. Much later Grierson spoke of him with great admiration, but at this time they had little in common. Grierson's claim that documentary 'allowed an adventure in the arts to assume the respectability of a public service' would not have appealed to Jennings, who saw the failings of public institution documentary ('the process and the chaps' Jennings used to call it). Grierson felt that Jennings was an intellectual dilettante. Certainly, at the height of the Depression, Jennings was working on a definitive edition of *Venus and Adonis* at Cambridge, then painting at St Tropez, while Grierson was producing *Drifters, Coalface, Shipyard* and *Industrial Britain*. Although Flaherty's film, for example, studiously avoids coming to terms with unemployment or the quality of industrial life, the contrast is obvious enough. It is of incidental interest that the documentaries of the thirties which in their photographic imagery most anticipate Jennings are Flaherty's *Industrial Britain* and Cavalcanti's *Coalface* – and that Jennings was to make several films in collaboration with Cavalcanti.

It may be that ultimately Jennings' relationship to the documentary movement was something like the relationship of a Ford, a Hawks or a Hitchcock to the Hollywood system. Like commercial American genres, documentary films tended to be made in certain formulas, to conform to certain basic rules. And just as Ford needed the Western as a form and the Western needed Ford's personal vision, so Jennings found a form in the propaganda documentary and enhanced the genre by his personal vision.

The differences between Grierson and Jennings are made explicit in their respective essays in the 1935 *Arts Today*. Grierson dismisses the 'trivialities' of the art of the cinema in favour of the use of film as educative propaganda: '. . . to create appreciation of public service and public purposes . . . to create a more imaginative and considered citizenship.' Jennings, writing about the theatre but in no way confining himself to it, bemoans the absence of poetry: 'I am aware that this continued defence of the poet is regarded as very dilettante by the now

politically-minded English. Art must now be social and useful.'
Jennings concludes his essay: 'For a short period at the end of
the sixteenth century and at the beginning of the seventeenth,
several Englishmen used the theatre as they found it, for their
own purposes of poetry and analysis of behaviour – *connais-
sance* – we have no word for it – naturally. That these may still
be constructed by Englishmen seems just a possibility. . . .' This
plea for the use of a public art for personal expression may
perhaps be taken as a statement of intent.

Jennings' first film as director and the only one he completed
before war began was *Spare Time* (1939). It was made for the
GPO Film Unit, but as a Mass Observation film, on 'the way
people spend their spare time'. Both the subject and the treatment reveal Jennings' concern with the Industrial Revolution
and its consequences. He chooses the three industries most
closely associated with the industrialisation of Britain – steel
(Sheffield), cotton (Manchester and Bolton, the home of
Crompton and workplace of Arkwright) and coal (Pontypridd)
– and seeks to observe both the industrial landscape, for its
vigour, beauty and drabness, and the quality of life within it.
The traditional documentarists attacked the film violently for
what they took to be satire and even 'cold disgust' in certain
sequences, especially the Kazoo Band. Why? Mass
Observation disliked the newspapers' assumptions about the
common man, their lip service to national feelings they really
knew little or nothing about, and tried to find out, however
crudely, what the common man really was thinking. It could be
said with some justice that many documentaries of the thirties,
rather like newspapers, stayed external to genuine attitudes.
Their ideas, like the dignity of labour, were not those of the
common man, but rather those of a Griersonian élite. Jennings'
Mass Observation background made him want to see beyond
the accepted public face and capture individuals and individual
feelings. *Spare Time* is a genuine, though personal, *observation*,
its tone emphasised by the sparse, non-committal, almost dry,
commentary.

Spare Time

In *Spare Time* there are also the beginnings of a personal style: a feeling for the industrial landscape of buildings and machinery, often portrayed in ambiguous beauty silhouetted against evening skies; a respect for the privacy of ordinary people coupled with the ability to give individuality even to those only briefly glimpsed; an eye for the single telling image (like the hobbling child) and the off-beat, most notably in the almost surreal appearance of the Kazoo Band in a recreation field amid grey terrace houses, but also in smaller observations in streets and houses. Speaking of Jennings' constant visual discoveries during the making of *Fires were Started*, William Sansom said 'Humphrey could be likened to an obsessive insect with antennae always alert and instantly sensitively selective, without human hum and ha, of what was needed'. He also revealed a talent for the complex organisation of material by editing, and for the use of music both as a unifying device and as an expression of life-styles (the Sheffield sequences are unified by brass band music, the Lancashire sequences by the Kazoo Band, the Welsh sequences by choral music).

The promise inherent in *Spare Time* was not immediately fulfilled in the initial war period 1939–40. Just as the 'phoney war' itself was uncertain, so the cinema was uncertain how best to serve the war effort. Documentary came under the bureaucratic control of the Ministry of Information and initially very little film was in production, despite the feeling among film-makers that the low national morale called for increased activity. Most of Jennings' short films at this time were assignments of more or less intractable material.

Speaking from America (1939) is a largely technical description, with diagrams, of the transatlantic telephone link, which served also as a radio link. Jennings was obviously interested in the technical process itself, but although the film is an efficient enough job it lacks much life. One remembers the images of the ragged and windswept lower Thames and the flat marshes, and the end of the film becomes a bit more interesting. Here, Jennings concentrates on the radio link and largely forgets the technical side of the operation. He introduces a characteristic image of sunlight behind clouds, then a shot of a man listening to his radio, ending simply with Roosevelt speaking of the United States as 'vital factors in world peace whether we choose it or not'.

S.S. Ionian (1939, also known as *Her Last Trip*) is about the role of merchant cargo ships, protected by the Royal Navy, in the Mediterranean. Despite an attempt (whether Jennings' or not is hard to say) to compare the ships' voyage to the Odyssey, the film is mostly very ordinary. One or two single images are interesting, notably the bizarre sight of a Gothic English cathedral in Cyprus, glimpsed through the ship's rigging in bright heat, and the film does convey an impression of the omnipresent strength of the Royal Navy. But *S.S. Ionian* returns to the Port of London and for a few brief moments at the end Jennings gives us, indulgently almost, a night sky over the Thames, the dark shapes of gasholders, chimneys, cranes, the moon over a sailing barge.

Welfare of the Workers (1940), about working conditions in wartime, is very much an assignment film and rather unmemorable. Yet even here Jennings' interest in the historical and industrial background of Britain manages to make itself felt. The war is seen as regressive and progressive at the same time. Regressive in that the workers are forced to abandon most of the rights won by the trades unions and the factory acts, a process which revives some of the worst aspects of the Industrial Revolution. This is emphasised by gloomy, almost claustrophobic images of factories. But also, paradoxically, the war is progressive: 'Compared with what she's used to,' says the film's commentary of a girl worker transferred to a factory in a cornfield, 'it's like stepping out of the nineteenth century into the twentieth.'

Spring Offensive (or *An Unrecorded Victory*) (1939), about the reclamation of East Anglian farmland for the war effort, provided material much closer to Jennings' interests. It was the landscape of his own upbringing and a subject to which he returned in *A Diary for Timothy*. The result was a much better film than most of the other early war shorts. *Spring Offensive* succeeds in impressing upon us the *totality* of war, reaching even these people, this landscape, affecting them vitally. After news of war, 'what will it mean to them?', as a farmer drains his glass of beer; 'what will it mean to the land?', as we see a field of sheaves of corn, dramatic music counterpointing the repose of the image. Jennings draws a nice parallel between the presence on the farm of a young evacuee and the reorganisation of farming – the boy arrives at the moment the BBC news announces the Government's plans. The film is full of image and music with a strong feeling for the beauty of the English countryside (and of respect for its 'most important crop – the English countryman') – men and horses in a misty landscape, a scarecrow and a harvester against a clear sky. This evocation of continuity with the past works well with the film's concluding comments, stressing the response of the land to the demands of war and striking a typically Jennings note of dark concern, that the land is properly looked after only in wartime – 'When peace comes, don't forget the land and its people again'. The final image is of dark trees beyond shadowy stooks of corn. But the film's feeling for the landscape is complicated by Jennings' interest in machinery; tractors and the vast steam rotary tiller, observed for their beauty and power, burst upon the pastoral scenes, giving a sense of war bringing the industrial revolution to the land. The tractors become both a complement to and an extension of the horses, and the steam engine churns the soil, frightening horses and game.

The importance attached to the radio is a dominant motif in all these early films, and one which persisted throughout the wartime films. Radio, in war, becomes a focal point of life. In *Spring Offensive* the BBC news is one of the most important events of the day and, as in *Welfare of the Workers*, there is a real sense of people taking direction from radio broadcasts. Radio is a dramatic device in that people depend on it for news of what is happening. It brings war into people's homes and becomes symbolic of the unity of a scattered people, as in *A Diary for Timothy*, when all the main characters' families listen intently to news of the Arnhem landing. In *Listen to Britain* radio is simply part of the fabric of life. In *The Silent Village* radio becomes the channel for enemy directions and information – and is abruptly switched off.

Perhaps Jennings' most interesting film of this period was *The First Days* (1939), a collaborative effort with Cavalcanti, Harry Watt and Pat Jackson. It is difficult to speculate about Jennings alone from the film, but it has stylistic and thematic concerns which recur in his later films. Its initial sequences show groups of people gathered round radios listening to the announcement of Britain's declaration of war. Unlike the other 1939–40 shorts, *The First Days* does not seek to explain, describe or state anything so much as to observe, like *Spare Time*, and from its observation catch a mood. The film lacks the closely woven texture of the later shorts, but its organisational structure of small impressions blended and juxtaposed to give a total impression must have appealed to Jennings. There are many observations in the film which encourage us to see his particular gifts for imagery at work: silent, empty streets while people listen intently to the radio; people hurrying to shelters while the siren wails; millions of sandbags 'rising like a tide in our streets'; empty picture frames at the National Gallery and emptiness in the British Museum; women knitting furiously; a barrage balloon over the Thames; gunners watching and waiting; a searchlight beam. The thematic concerns too: friendliness and good humour; the mood of jovial resistance masking anxious determination ('people joked, but in their hearts was devastation'); the sacrifice of separation from loved ones (the fine sequence of the girl and the flower-seller, ending with the camera picking up a new, unknown man in uniform, universalising the private moment); the strangeness of a 'new world' (one side of a street 'sunny and civilised', the other – the camera panning across to a line of tanks in the shadows of trees

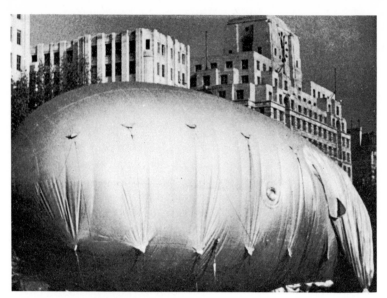

A strange new world (*The First Days*)

– like 'a convoy in France'; or London mothers remarking on the quietness when their children have been evacuated). A sense of threat everywhere underlies the jovial mood in the 'city of shadows' where, 'on the darkest night the gleaming river may betray London yet'. The very last images express this threat: sandbags and guards at the Palace, a barrage balloon, the King and Queen looking up, the balloon rising, the music reaching its climax and the image darkening.

Jennings responded very quickly, artistically and personally, to the war and his response seems to have been analogous to that of the new generation who went into uniform, finding as *The First Days* says 'that they lived in a world without peace'. A central impulse in Jennings' war films is the deeply felt realisation of living in 'a strange new world' in which certain manifestations of civilisation are endangered. The consciousness of this is a primary source of passion in the films.

Films for the war effort

The bulk of Jennings' films belong to the general documentary propaganda war effort. This meant that like other film-makers he worked at great speed and under government supervision. That Jennings' films have survived so much better than others already implies that they were distinctive and perhaps essentially different in kind. After *London Can Take It* (1940), Jennings' particular gifts seem to have been recognised, not least by his enthusiastic producer, Ian Dalrymple, and it may be that he was given more freedom than some of his colleagues. Almost all documentaries were different from the commercially shown newsreels whose commentaries were full of savage chauvinism, references to 'the mark of the Hun' and so forth. What remains of such sentiments in the documentaries is toned down and made more reflective, but as far as one can tell Jennings' films went further than any others in avoiding the statement of explicit attitudes to the enemy. He was not a pacifist but he was more interested in how people behaved under duress and how the collective spirit of resistance evoked Britain's traditional civilisation. His films show arms production and servicemen in a state of readiness, but attack or retaliation itself is marginal to his work. The only weapons seen in action are for defensive purposes and most of the defenders are civilians. As *London Can Take It* puts it, 'these civilians are good soldiers'.

Most war documentaries were made to fulfil very precise functions: to advise or reassure people or explain events. Films like *Squadron 992*, *Merchant Seamen*, *Coastal Command* or *Ferry Pilot* (many of them made with the technicians Jennings used) show men doing jobs, like many documentaries of the thirties. Jennings does not seem to have been interested in such projects, although *Fires were Started* has elements of this approach. Even in his earlier, conventional assignments, one senses the attempt to open the subjects out, to make them speak for more than their immediate function. Most of the later war films, and especially the 1940–41 shorts, avoid descriptive narrative and explanation and become observation, evocation, meditation. Their special qualities were not perhaps so apparent at the time. *Listen to Britain* was hailed as a 'worthy box-office successor' to *Ferry Pilot* and *Target for Tonight*, yet its fluidity, its imaginative association could hardly be more different from the stiff, prosaic narrative of the other two films.

As propaganda Jennings' films lack the precise functional objectives which were the rule, partly because they are concerned with subtleties of national mood and morale and partly because they are Jennings' own transformations of what he actually observed. Grierson, a man obsessed with social use, found *London Can Take It* (made for export to the United States) a beautiful film. It 'revealed enormous sympathy for England and so far so good. The question is whether creating sympathy necessarily creates confidence'. And Grierson may be right. The film is moving and sympathetic but the creation of confidence does not seem its main purpose. The same could be said for almost all of Jennings' war films. *Fires were Started* was about the Auxiliary Fire Service when it had ceased to exist, about the blitz when it had passed. Amid the pressing needs of wartime one might have expected a film about the National Fire Service, with a direct contemporary reference, and probably also a different kind of film. Grierson, after Jennings' death, called him a 'rare one' in the documentary group: 'He was one fighting ... for the right to contemplate, and this in a period not easily given over to such.'

In mood and structure *The First Days* seems to have been the main antecedent of Jennings' remarkable sequence of short films of 1940–41. At the time of *Spring Offensive* Jennings was apparently not yet wholly committed to film, though he wanted to contribute what he could to the war effort. *London Can Take It* was his first public success and seems to have been the decisive experience. After it one can scarcely doubt, seeing the films, his artistic commitment to film, and the striking of recurrent attitudes and the characteristic feeling for construction and choice of image begin to appear.

London Can Take It (again a collaborative effort, with Harry Watt) had its genesis in a despatch by Quentin Reynolds, war correspondent of the American *Collier's Weekly*. Library and newly shot material was assembled round the words to show Americans what London was like in the Blitz. Jennings probably liked Reynolds' observations and his matter-of-fact style of delivery, but despite the film's origin it was here that Jennings began to discover fully the relationship of sound and image and image to image, as well as the emotive force of individual images. Reynolds' own style is important and the film takes perhaps less extravagant creative risks than Jennings' more personal works, but *London Can Take It* is nevertheless unmistakably Jennings, his first real evocation of the British people not so much at war as living with war.

The film is given shape by the natural progression from evening through to morning and the beginning of another working day. In between is the 'strange new world' of the Blitz, with its constant contrasts of the ordinary and the extraordinary, the casual and the tense, beauty and destruction, stillness and action, silence and noise, light and dark. First it is evening: people return from work; peace reigns in sunlit streets; a last glimmer of light glows on a Georgian terrace. As people queue for shelters, the pace becomes less casual and the film cuts away to the silhouettes of searchlight and gun crews, their machines pointing skyward, turning slowly, waiting, silent. The sky becomes the focus of attention. To the accompaniment of the siren we see a bright evening sky over London, with just one dark cloud, then dark skies are intercut with the machines of the watch. Before the first explosion, after Reynolds' sober 'Here they come', Jennings holds a shot of a dark sky with one long, bright gash in the clouds, as the roar of engines increases, as if expecting a thunderbolt from heaven. Then come blackness and the first explosion, introducing the interplay of shadowy darkness and the sudden illumination of guns and men, buildings, wardens chatting easily, fires and firemen. There is the briefest of shots in which an explosion momentarily lights

80

Beauty and destruction (*London Can Take It*)

up the dome of St Paul's, which opens the film and recurs throughout. While explosions and fire-fighting continue, Jennings cuts away to a man rocking in a hammock, men playing darts, a family sleeping. Finally the wail of the siren introduces dawn – the Thames, the Houses of Parliament in mist, people surveying the damage thoughtfully or casually, going off to work as usual, carrying on amid the debris.

Bronowski says he learnt from Jennings that 'a clown or a poet can impose his macabre sense of fun on the imagination merely by treating extravagance as normal' and moments of this film (the bus thrown up, stranded almost, beside a wrecked house, or the woman entering the shop by its shattered window) remind us of this, as do similar moments in other Jennings films. Towards the end, Reynolds' '... and they'll kill thousands of people' is accompanied by the shot of a cat being passed carefully out of the ruins of a house. Jennings' use of

81

London Can Take It

sound is already masterly. The commentary is used alongside images which complicate our responses rather than illustrate the words. It is at the service of both the images and natural sounds, lapsing when for example the drone of approaching bombers creates all the necessary atmosphere. On the whole, the images tend to make the general sentiments of the words more concrete and particular: the jaunty, wounded warden who gets a light from a man in a taxi *is* 'the unconquerable spirit and courage of the people of London'.

Stylistically, the progress from *London Can Take It* to *Listen to Britain* shows an increasing concern for the non-narrative formal organisation of material and an increasing desire to move away from the specific language of commentary. Both moves liberate Jennings, make him more free to make his own connections.

An important element in this development was the increasing reliance on natural sounds but particularly on music. Music was already an integral formal element in *Spare Time*, for Jennings was always a great lover of music. On one level it was an aspect of his public images and his faith in popular culture: Welsh choral music (*Spare Time, The Silent Village*), popular songs (*Listen to Britain, Fires were Started, The True Story of Lilli Marlene*), military brass band music (*Listen to Britain*), dance music, street barrel-organ music and so on. But, as Vaughan Williams stresses in *Dim Little Island*, serious music was also immensely popular in wartime, both English music (Purcell, Vaughan Williams, Elgar, Handel) and German (Beethoven, Mozart, Haydn). English music tended to heighten the sense of Englishness, of course, but all classical music is used by Jennings as both a reminder and a source of civilised human values at a time when they threatened to be submerged by barbarism. Myra Hess' Mozart in *Listen to Britain*, at first a counterpoint to the images of threat in the National Gallery, is carried over to shots of everyday events outside, its soaring quality endowing those events with human dignity, like the Handel at the end of *Words for Battle*. Beethoven accompanies bombed out buildings in *Heart of Britain* and one of the most desperate sequences in *A Diary for Timothy*, providing both passion and irony.

Heart of Britain (1941) continues Jennings' meditation on Britain's traditions, given a special significance and dignity by war. In Coventry, 'the everyday tasks of women came right through the fire and became heroic'; for others, 'the simplest, most difficult task of all was just staying put with war round the corner'. But the film emphasises continuity with the past, playing with the paradox that 'the winds of war' have reached the innermost parts of the heart of Britain, yet 'the heart of Britain remains unmoved, unchangeable'. The initial implication that the 'heart of Britain is its countryside is progressively complicated by the juxtaposed imagery of cities, spires, chimneys, black Sheffield, imposing a sense of the indivisibility of the contrasting elements of Britain, nicely caught in the metaphor of 'the valleys of power and the rivers of industry'. The film makes effective use of commentary but gains even greater force and fluency when music replaces words. Firstly Beethoven ('the genius of the Germany that was'), played by the Hallé Orchestra, is carried over to shots of bombed churches and houses in Coventry, including the remarkable image, possibly from newsreel, of a dark curtain billowing out in the foreground of a row of bombed buildings. Even more powerfully, the Huddersfield Choir's 'Hallelujah Chorus' ('People who sing like that in times like these cannot be beaten') is continued over shots of people in ruined streets and industry. Introduced by 'No one with impunity troubles the heart of Britain', the chorus then soars over a complex sequence of concluding images (pilots and planes, spires, a plane being towed out of its hangar, countryside, more spires, a rocky hillside, plane propellers whirring with cockpit closing, a distant river, a plane taking off). The sequence reminds us that while Jennings' images are concrete, they also combine to create from the concrete elements a spiritual abstraction of 'the heart of Britain'.

In keeping with Jennings' ideas about the role of personal invention in art, *London Can Take It* used an existing and probably famous despatch. *Words for Battle* (1941) applies well-known literary quotations (though some of the particular choices – and the absence of Shakespeare – are puzzling) to the contemporary situation. The movement of the film is to re-interpret and give concrete form to the words, from Camden's description of Britannia through Milton's 'Areopagitica' (the tradition of liberty and tolerance, with Spitfires and airmen as the 'eagle mewing her mighty youth' and the Nazis as 'those that love the twilight'), Blake's *Jerusalem* (the evacuation of children), Browning's *Home Thoughts* ('How can I help England?'), Kipling's *When the English began to hate* (blitz damage and death), to Churchill and Lincoln's Gettysburg Address. Sound and image combine to alter our perspective of both. Churchill's 'We shall never surrender' accompanies an image

From the end of *Words for Battle*

of St Paul's towering above a mass of rubble, and the speech's reference to the New World introduces Lincoln, whose words 'that the Government of the people, by the people, and for the people, shall not perish from the earth' accompany a misty Parliament Square with trees, people passing and tanks rumbling past the Lincoln memorial. The purpose of the film becomes completely apparent only at the end, when the noise of tanks and Handel's *Water Music* (which introduces and punctuates the film) take over the soundtrack. The film becomes wordless, and the final images follow the faces of ordinary men and women, in and out of uniform, while the music and noise reach their climax. The values and the greatness implicit in the quotations is transferred to the ordinary people who represent continuity with the past and are both the source and the embodiment of its values. The effect is irresistible.

Listen to Britain (1941) is the climax, both stylistically and thematically, to the first phase of Jennings' development in film. It avoids personal invention in the form of commentary by relying entirely on natural sounds and, towards the end, music. The spoken introduction does not seem to be integral to the film and serves to show how much the images and sounds lose in richness when verbalised.

It is a most unwarlike film. Its basic motivation is a balance between menace (to a culture rather than to material things) on the one hand and harmony and continuity from the past on the other. Images of menace are constantly juxtaposed with images of the population's reactions. Almost all images gain complete meaning only when seen in context. Thus, the fighter planes fly over harvesters and gunners in the fields, working side by side; the sandbags, empty frames and fire-buckets at the National Gallery are intercut both with steady tracking shots of the calm faces of the audience or shots of people eating sandwiches or looking at paintings and accompanied by Mozart; inside the blacked-out train, Canadian soldiers sing and talk; Big Ben stands dark and scaffolded but London calls the world through the BBC foreign service; a woman watches children at play, looks at a photograph of her soldier son; the sound of tanks and trucks introduces a convoy rumbling through a sunny, half-timbered village; and so on. Frequently the sequence of images acts as a reminder of the interdependence and essentiality of people's functions (emphasised by the constant overlapping of sound, sequences usually being introduced first by sounds): the colliers are followed by the train sequence; the aero factory is followed by planes taking off; the girl factory workers give way to groups of servicewomen waiting at a station, and they in turn are followed by the ambulance service group. This dialectical montage has the effect of constantly complicating and expanding our consciousness of the individual shots so that, for example, the faintly ludicrous 'Ash Grove' sequence is suddenly given immense poignancy by the shot of the women's helmets.

86

With the elimination of commentary, the images or sequences often acquire a rich ambiguity which is a constant feature of Jennings' style (reminding us that Jennings was a product of the I. A. Richards school of criticism that produced Empson's conception of the ambiguity or multiplicity of the poetic statement). The meaning of an image, or more frequently the connections between images, are left to the audience's emotions for interpretation (unlike Eisenstein's montage which implies a precise intellectual connection). The blacked-out engine halted in dark countryside, then grinding slowly forward, dark moonlight glinting on metallic surfaces (part of a sequence but here having an inner dynamism within the single shot too) can be both menacing and symbolic of immense power (as locomotives usually are in Jennings); the Blackpool dancers, wedged between two shots of the watchers on the dark shore, can be either gay or desperate. Like *Heart of Britain*, *Listen to Britain* also expresses Jennings' sense of the indivisibility of Britain, not only of task but of landscape, especially the pastoral and the industrial. At one moment, as in the dissolve from birdsong and the wooded ridge at dawn to the sound of steps on cobbles and a grimy industrial landscape, the two are made to coalesce; at another, in the stunningly abrupt cut from hissing steam to shimmering, silent trees, they simply exist simultaneously. The justly famous final sequences of *Listen to Britain*, like the ending of the two previous films, soar into an expression of the unity of Britain at war. Flanagan and Allen at a factory canteen merge into the Myra Hess concert (Friday, 13 June) at the National Gallery. Then Mozart is carried over to accompany a series of 'public' images outside (trees, a barrage balloon, St Martin-in-the-Fields, people boarding buses, Nelson, a sailor, the National Gallery across Trafalgar Square) and, more audaciously, a tank factory, where the music is lost imperceptibly in the noise. The factory noises dissolve into brass band music, which introduces a street parade and continues over Blakean images of a steel mill. Out of the noise of the mill emerges the only 'unnatural' sound of the

Listen to Britain

film – a massed choir singing 'Rule Britannia', uniting the juxtaposed shots of factories and cornfields. 'Rule Britannia' is the only sound whose source is not identified in the film. The inevitable effect is that it seems to well out from *all* the elements of the film. Jennings' feelings for unity and 'the spirit of England' here found their most tumultuous expression.

After developing a distinctively associative and non-narrative style in the 1941 shorts, Jennings began work on *Fires were Started* (*I was a Fireman*) (1943), which seems at first sight both less complex and less concerned with formal values. This is largely because the film has a basic linear, narrative, dramatic structure which has to take account of plot and individual characters (and the film is about its individuals to an extent that the later *A Diary for Timothy* is not). Up to *Fires were Started* Jennings' films had not sought to explore character or dramatic relationships and their form seems to have been imposed almost entirely at the editing stage. *Fires were Started*, however, needed narrative development and character study, so that Jennings had to have ideas about the shape and movement of the film while shooting it. William Sansom (Barrett in the film) has said that the actors knew nothing of the basic scheme of the film, that all dialogue was made up on the spot and that there was constant distraction during shooting. For the important 'Please don't talk about me' sequence the tune decided upon was, apparently, the result of five minutes' general discussion. In these conditions it is remarkable that formal concerns are, in fact, as important in *Fires were Started* as anywhere else in Jennings. Indeed it is partly because of these formal concerns that the film avoids the utilitarian ordinariness of other war documentaries and remains a masterpiece today.

Only partly, however, for *Fires were Started* is also Jennings' best and most individualised evocation of the personal qualities of ordinary people – their courage, their humanity towards others, their unquestioning and determined commitment to a group task, the film stressing the men's feelings as members of a group rather than their individually different temperaments. Jennings returned to the time of the Blitz, two years before, for his best exploration of these qualities. The actors, all seconded firemen, were glad to work on the film because this was a period without much bombing. The film was about the Blitz and the Auxiliary Fire Service but made when both had become history. The Blitz itself had almost certainly already acquired an aura of heroic myth. This must have suited Jennings' purposes, for the film is reflective, even nostalgic, about a particular moment in time. Perhaps the film's propagandist purpose was indeed to act as a reminder of people's own grandeur.

Fires were Started certainly works partly on the level of epic myth. Even more than in the 1940–41 films, the Blitz is seen as something akin to a great natural disaster. The very title, recall-

Fire and water (*Fires Were Started*)

ing Blake and a phrase much used in BBC news bulletins, seems chosen to discourage the notion of some human enemy agency starting the fires. The firemen, despite their awareness of the munitions ship in the dock, show no real interest in the enemy, who seems unimportant. They simply prepare, wait and go into action when called upon. The film has a symbolic dimension which helps to explain why the imagery of man with and against the elements of fire and water is dwelt upon with such force. The symbolic dimension reminds us again of Jennings' interest in the Tarot pack. Apart from the Chariot, the other card-image which inspired him was the Maison-Dieu, the house struck by fire from heaven. It was one of Jennings' key images long before the Blitz made the symbol actual. Like Blake, Jennings conceived history as the realisation of human imaginings, and the final test of an image or symbolic situation was that it must produce itself as an actual historical event.

This conviction, combined with the fact that the Maison-Dieu, like the Chariot, belong in the Tarot pack to the four 'elements of cosmic fatality', helps to explain the sense of fatality which pervades *Fires were Started*. Though it is generally assumed to be of sinister import, the Maison-Dieu's origins and precise symbolic value are obscure. Tarot symbols always had both a figurative and a symbolic meaning and an analogy for the Maison-Dieu has been made with the alchemists' furnace, which had to receive a tongue of fire from heaven, at which the imprudent who could not foresee it were thunderstruck. It is worth remembering that the science of alchemy, which aimed at the union of opposites, was not purely physical. Its ultimate goal was the Philosopher's Stone and it exacted the highest intellectual and moral qualities. Consideration of these symbolic associations can tell us much about Jennings' deepest feelings about the impact of war on the British people and their response.

An examination of the various stages of the film reveals its highly formal structure; one is tempted to call them acts or movements by analogy with theatre or music. The morning sequences introduce us both to the men and to the organisation of the Auxiliary Fire Service within which they function. Our knowledge of this establishes 14Y and, more particularly the 'crazy gang', as only a small part of a large organisation, a fact of which we are constantly reminded. The life of the men and the sub-station is shown as easy and good-humoured but there is also a feeling of unreality, almost of dream, about it, brought out especially by such vivid fleeting moments as that of the flute-player, the tree in blossom, or the dog asleep in the sun. In the afternoon and evening sequences, one becomes increasingly aware of Jennings' control of shape and mood. While Johnny Daniels and Barrett look round the docks, they see a sailing barge with its sails billowing, the image's lyrical quality emphasised by the music. Later there is a dissolve from a barrage balloon rising from a barge to Jacko asleep at 14Y. As the evening draws on the men's recreation and preparation are

An early sequence from *Fires Were Started*

counterpointed by increasingly frequent cut-aways to the river, ever more dark, mysterious, menacing and – paradoxically – beautiful. Sound adds another dimension: Barrett's rhumba music is continued over shots of the dark river (the effect beautifully undercut by the cut back to Johnny and B. A. Brown dancing ponderously to it); the siren accompanying the end of 'One man went to mow' is carried over to dark cranes and rigging, an A.A. gun turning; Rumbold's 'O eloquent just and mighty death' accompanies a shot of dark sky. Jennings' procedure in these sequences has the effect of a fatal drawing together of the defenders and what they will defend, giving them a quality of predestination. After the fire-call, defenders and defended are merged.

Initially the fire-fighting itself is treated naturalistically and concentrates on action, though the frightened horse introduces a different note. But Jacko's death and the events which follow

93

Fires Were Started

are given a very formal, almost abstract, treatment: the close-up of the rope slipping through Jacko's fingers, Jacko amid flames and falling, the hose flicking loose, dark smoke, Johnny's expression as he looks up, the shot from the other side of the river of a mushroom of fire, followed by blackness. The treatment here depersonalises the event and suggests an almost ritual sacrifice. This distancing is emphasised by the subsequent cut back to control headquarters, placing the event in its wider context and giving us a less involved view of things (this is also the function of the shots of the observer post on the other side of the river).

After the arrival of standby reinforcements at 14Y ('You people seem to be having a regular pasting tonight' – 'Yes, our boys are at the docks'), the film cuts back to fire-fighting, but the mood has changed. The fire, having claimed its victim, is in the process of being mastered. Whereas before great difficulty was experienced in pointing the hoses down into the fire, now many shots show the men working above the fire, hosing down into the flames. The editing rhythm becomes less urgent and the music, level and controlled, evokes a continuing struggle which demands only perseverance. At dawn there is a grey, weary mood. The men are conscious of the loss of Jacko, though this again is counterpointed by the chirpiness of men from other units and by the typically Jennings gay girl with wild hair who opens up the mobile canteen. As the men 'knock off and make up', shots tend to avoid faces and concentrate on hands, hoses, legs and water: the action over, the men begin to become aware of the events of the night. The men move off slowly over the rubble as the streets begin to fill up with people off to work.

Like so much else in the film, the whole treatment of Jacko has a discreetly fatalistic quality, linked with the initiation of Barrett. Only in Jacko's case is there a cut back to his wife, alone, after his introduction. In the afternoon and evening sequences the shots of river and sky frequently cut back to Jacko and there is a moment when the sub tells Barrett he will

Jacko's death: sequence from *Fires Were Started* ▶

be all right just as Jacko enters the room. In the series of close-ups on the way to the fire Jacko alone is haloed by fire. After Jacko's death, as the work continues, Barrett, for the first time, takes part in the actual fire-fighting, appearing alongside Rumbold, Jacko's partner 'up top', and it is Barrett again who finds Jacko's helmet. Back at 14Y (where Jennings refuses any exploitation of the fact that Jacko is gone) Barrett is no longer an outsider: Eileen brings in six mugs of tea, the right number now; she calls him Bill and he calls her Mum. In the structure of the film it is almost as if Barrett's integration depends on Jacko's death.

The fate of the munitions ship is also integral to the sacrifice of Jacko. As the men arrive for work at the start they are aware, and made aware, of the ship being loaded. Later, Johnny shows it to Barrett – 'Ain't she a smasher, cock, eh?', and the foreman is overheard saying the ship will be ready on time. After the cut-aways to the ship during the evening, both of these observations are picked up next morning: asked if they have had a bad night, Johnny says the unharmed ship is a 'sight for sore eyes'; when Jacko's wife, unaware of her husband's death, stops listening to the news, the film dissolves to the foreman saying they will make it all right. Finally, Jacko's funeral, in the presence of all the team, including the injured Sub-Officer, Eileen and Mrs Jackson, is intercut with the munitions ship moving downstream, the trumpet of a last post blossoming forth into triumphant music. The final dissolve, rather than cut, between the six men and the bows of the ship makes Jennings' feelings about their relationship quite clear.

Denis Forman has said with justice that 'one knows instinctively that *Fires were Started* can never lose its strength'. Although particularised in time and place, the film's formal and symbolic qualities, together with its humanity, give it a universal significance outside of time. It is the masterpiece not only of Jennings but also of the British documentary school and the whole British cinema.

The blending of documentary with fiction and narrative tech-

98

After the fire (*Fires Were Started*)

Fires Were Started: the final dissolve

niques in *Fires were Started* was continued in Jennings' next
two films, *The Silent Village* (1943) and *The True Story of Lilli
Marlene* (1944). *Fires were Started* had been well received and
Jennings must still have had freedom to choose subjects to
which he was attracted. *The Silent Village* is the story of
Lidice, the Czechoslovak mining village wiped out by the Germans, set in a similar Welsh mining village. Jennings had a
particular fondness for Welsh miners, and the idea of setting a
story of resistance unto death in defence of a civilised and
industrious way of life in a Welsh mining village where he saw
those same qualities obviously had a strong appeal for him. *The
Silent Village* is a moving and often beautifully composed film,
but it lacks dramatic dynamism. Its dramatic shortcomings are
emphasised by its almost completely static shots and its exces-
sive use of choral music. Jennings' films as a whole are often
criticised for the static quality of their images, though in other

Jennings directing Welsh miners (above); and the anonymous loudspeaker (*The Silent Village*)

films, when conditions allowed, he makes extensive and effective use of pan and travelling shots. *The Silent Village* is also a very impersonal film, the tribute of an outside sympathiser rather than of one involved.

Jennings' talent was in observing actuality, but here we get his *idea* of what occupation might be like. Much more than in his other films we learn little of what the villagers are like, perhaps because they also do not know what occupation would really mean. While the observation of village life is sympathetic, the film is much less successful in observing both the details of occupation and the actors playing Germans. Even so, *The Silent Village* is interesting in a number of ways, not least for what it says of people's response to the Industrial Revolution. At one point, the film dissolves from a miners' meeting about silicosis to an open landscape of fields, and the film constantly reminds us of the village's dependence on the pit. The people, however, accept work with dignity and a consciousness of its potential for comradeship and social life in general. The film is interesting too in the way it shows the threatened villagers thrown back on their past – the ruined fortress in the hills and the desire to preserve their traditional culture. Stylistically successful are the sudden introductions of the impersonal, anonymous loudspeaker on the Nazi car after the long, warm sequences of the village at work and play, or the symbolic use of natural elements: the changing moods of the river (the river itself symbolic of the life-force) and the sudden onset of winter as the oppression reaches its height.

Lilli Marlene is in some ways a more interesting film, but equally, I think, a failure. Like *The Silent Village* its fault lies in the extremely conventional treatment of Germans which verges on (unintentional, I am sure) caricature. The contrast between Jennings' Germans and the brief newsreel shots of Von Paulus after Stalingrad, for example, is most telling. The failure to integrate extreme theatricality – many sequences are obviously studio-staged and some shots strangely over-decorated – and raw newsreel is one of the basic faults of the

The True Story of Lilli Marlene

film. The other is the narrative structure, the faithful following through of the story of the song. The subject probably needed a more generally imaginative and non-narrative approach. The possibilities of such an approach are suggested only briefly: the broadcasting of tender greetings over dirty and weary German soldiers or of a German announcement as British soldiers listen. And the film fails to explore sufficiently some of the most interesting things about the song, either the unconscious irony of the popularity of this most sentimental and romantic of songs among soldiers in the direst conditions, or the successive transformations the song underwent. Even so, it is not hard to see why Jennings was interested in the origins and history of a song that caught the popular wartime imagination of opposed armies through the medium of radio, and – like *The Silent Village* – *Lilli Marlene* has its moments: men listening to the song round the glow of a radio dial in the desert night, the use of newsreel in the desert offensive, or the almost soaring sequence as the song accompanies the Italian invasion. Best of all, typically, are the final sequences of 'the London docks on a Saturday night in peacetime'. Jennings foresaw that the song would achieve a permanent symbolic significance, and these concluding moments, projecting into a peaceful future reflecting on its wartime past, show much of the qualities of life that Britain was defending: lively, noisy friendliness, ordinary people going about their everyday tasks, barrel-organ music playing, and an ex-Eighth Army soldier smoking quietly in the doorway of his shop (a corner tobacconist's, like Jacko's in *Fires were Started*), while inside his wife copes with the children.

Lilli Marlene is the most fabricated of all Jennings' films and *The Silent Village* one of his most static. Taken together they suggest that he would not have been happy making feature films in the commercial system. That his true talent, in accord with his own aesthetic theories, lay in the observation and transformation of *real* elements seems supported by the little-known short film *The 80 Days*, also made in 1944, about the V1 attacks on Southern England. The pervading sense of external threat that the Blitz provided had been missing in the middle war years but now returned, and *The 80 Days* is acutely conscious of this: the commentary speaks of the people being 'tested for a second time' and not flinching. To a large extent the film reverts to the style of the earlier shorts, sharing with them a sparse use of commentary and a reliance on the power of natural sounds (the long-held buzz or grumble of a doodlebug making its inexorable journey to the heart of London) and of music (the music from the weary dawn sequences of *Fires were Started* begins softly after the explosion of the bomb and the spreading of smoke across the city, seen in the distance, the shot held for a long time). Here, too, are the same forceful and intimate observations of ordinary people, the same striking imagery of men and their weapons, the same sense of humor (the boys smoking in the field, and even the men playing bowls while the bombs pass overhead), the same talent for the single strikingly symbolic image, like the rescue worker who purposefully hitches up his pants at the end. Other elements are new. The battle of London is seen as part of the battle for France and the mood of the people has changed. 'The grim and gay defiance of the old Blitz days was gone, people were tired.' Determination remains but has become more sombre. For almost the first time in Jennings we are made acutely aware of apprehension, suffering and death.

A Diary for Timothy (1944–5) also returns to the associative style of the 1941 shorts but pushes it to its limits. There is narrative in the sense that there are characters and movement forward in time but there is no plot. *A Diary for Timothy* depends for its effect on highly formal organisation and associative montage. Sequences of images rather than individual shots are striking. What is almost a description of Jennings' method can be found in a passage that he intended to include in *Pandemonium*, a description of an impression or image from Faraday's Diary: 'A combination of many effects, each utterly insensible alone, into one sum of fine effect.'

The film is formally split into six sections, each ending with a fade to blackness. Basically, the first half of the film (September to October) traces the slow waning of hope; the central passage (November) stands still, meditates; then the second half (December to the New Year) follows the build-up of hope through Christmas and the Russian offensive. The overall pattern of fall and rise has a remarkable symmetry. The formal unity of the film is stressed in many ways, working as it does to and from a number of constant points of reference – the lives of Alan the farmer, Peter the wounded pilot, Goronwy the miner, Bill the engineer and Tim himself, the passing of time and the changes of weather, radio bulletins, the clearing of mines from the beaches, the haunting musical theme.

A Diary for Timothy reveals Jennings' associative style at its most developed and, intellectually if not emotionally, its most difficult. A good example is the sequence following the news of

News of the Arnhem landing: sequence from *A Diary for Timothy* ▶

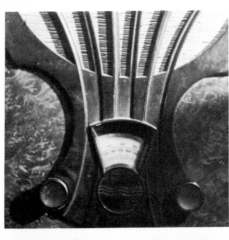

the Arnhem landing: the radio report links the families of Goronwy and Bill, Tim's mother and Alan, all listening intently, stopping what they are doing; from Alan's thoughtful face, already accompanied by the piano music of the Appassionata Sonata, the images move to Dame Myra Hess and her audience; a passage about rain from the Arnhem report fades in and out again as the music gets louder and the images shift to rain falling on a street reservoir, then to bombed roofs and repair workers and back to hands at the piano. With the wet reflection of a pit-head and 'Rain, too much rain', the film launches into a further sequence of images and events: Tim's mother writing Christmas cards, rain on Bill's engine, rain in the fields, Tim's baptism, Peter learning to walk again, Goronwy brought up from the pit on a stretcher. It is of course possible to attempt an intellectual analysis of the sequence of images but such analysis rarely takes us far enough. Jennings seems to have reached such a pitch of personal freedom in his association of ideas and shifts of mood that we lose the precise significance of the movement of the film and respond almost completely emotionally. Such sequences, for all their essential mystery, are successful. For example, the long-delayed cut from Bill peering grimly into dark fog through his cabin window to 'loveliness, whiteness, Christmas day' which the commentary has already announced. Elsewhere, as in the brief central passage – London, the gravediggers scene from *Hamlet*, the rescue workers – the artifice shows through and the effect is less happy.

It does seem that Jennings had reached some kind of impasse. The extreme elaboration of form and the structural and symbolic use of characters (who are never given the intimately human dimension of the men in *Fires were Started* or even of minor figures in earlier shorts) suggest a feeling of both isolation and despair. It is interesting that *A Diary for Timothy* marks a return to a central use of commentary. Despite the occasional extravagant phrase that suits the film's mood ('and death came by telegram to many of us on

'Loveliness, whiteness, Christmas Day': (*A Diary for Timothy*)

Christmas Eve'), the commentary often gets close to pathos and certainly verbalises sentiments one would have expected Jennings to prefer unspoken. For Jennings, all this hints at a possible decline of creative confidence.

The grim mood already apparent in *The 80 Days* is overpowering in *A Diary for Timothy*. The threat here is not the external one of bombs falling but internal – the morale of people after five years of war and long separation from loved ones. The war has grown old: the mines on the beaches get mixed up with barbed wire. Even the constant shifts of mood seem to indicate a war which has become a habit. Moments of joy like Christmas morning fail to offset the prevailing disillusion, which emerges so strongly from the 'Rain, too much rain' sequence, full of pain, injury, separation. The film was completed when victory was assured yet even the New Year sequences of the Russian offensive and the Allied advance conclude on a sombre note. Goronwy, worrying about the future, and Bill go back to 'everyday life, and everyday danger'. In the final images Tim yelling is intercut with bombs falling, and in a long dissolve his face on the pillow emerges from the flames. The commentary tells him it's only chance that he is safe and asks what he will do about the world while he bites his hands, giving his face an anxious expression. He throws his arms out in a defiant gesture as the music reaches a crescendo but then the screen goes black and the crescendo gives way to the melancholy, unresolved solo violin music with which the film began. In these last images and sounds – challenging but ambiguous, purposely confused – one senses very strongly, as one does throughout *A Diary for Timothy*, Jennings' fears for the values that war had sustained and his doubts about the kind of world that peace would bring.

Doubts about peace – the post-war films
Jennings' anxieties about the coming of peace were perhaps only partly social. *A Diary for Timothy* is about a crisis of national morale, but for Jennings the film-maker it also represents a crisis of style and subject matter. During the war he saw his ideas and feelings about British civilisation and genius given an actuality from which he was able to create his best films. Richard Winnington recalls Jennings telling him 'firmly and passionately, that good films could only be made in times of disaster'. Jennings' own attitudes survived into peace-time, but in peacetime how was he to find a context in which to express them?

The problem is posed by his first post-war film, *A Defeated People* (1945), which is about life in Germany and the government of the British Army. The film sets out to reconcile the opposed attitudes, of pity and vengeance, to a defeated Germany, but the need to describe administrative organisation gave Jennings a subject much less flexible than the British war films. In consequence the film seems broken-backed. The sequences about administration are dull and unsubtle, except

110

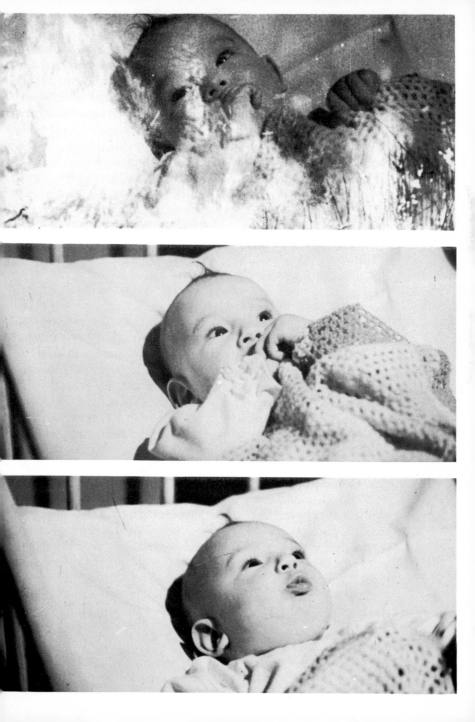

perhaps for the final intercutting of judges taking the oath and sunlit children at play. By contrast, the opening sequences about the destruction of cities and communications and the stirring of the 'life-force' are both subtle and sympathetic. What the film says about defeated Germans – 'our power of destruction is terrible but the will to live is still stronger' – could have been said about Britons at war; and to show the stirring of life amid the ruins he turns to barrel organ music, family feeling, children at play and the dignity of the banal, everyday acts of living. Despite its passages of interest, however, it is hard to see in *A Defeated People* very much of the author of the great British war films.

The Cumberland Story (1947) provided a subject – 'a pioneer effort in the reorganisation of British coalfields' – closer to his interests, and it is a more successful film. Visually it has little of the excitement and complexity of the war films, despite some nice observations and the use of the sea for its imagery of potential calm and violence. Intellectually, though, it belongs in the mainstream of his thought about the Industrial Revolution's genius and daring and its social consequences. The film is organised round the pioneering imagination of the past (in the form of an early nineteenth-century plan for an undersea pit), and daring and vision in the present (in the person of an expert sent to revitalise the industry, as well as in the miners themselves). The main obstacle to progress is the miners' consciousness of past exploitation and present demoralisation, their attitudes shaped by the desperate 1930s. The expert says the men are obsessed with the past and must look forward; but, typically for Jennings, part of the film is the expert's increasing appreciation of the force of the past for the men. The propagandist purpose of *The Cumberland Story* is the achievement of harmony for the future. All the same, Jennings' touch is most sure when evoking the mood of the past and its continuing effect in the present.

Jennings made only two more films before his death in 1950. Both *Dim Little Island* and *Family Portrait* signal a return to

Past and future (*The Cumberland Story*)

an earlier style and the subject of the national mood and temperament. In the late 1940s, however, he worked on a projected film about the London Symphony Orchestra. Only his 'working sketches' remain but they are of considerable interest and suggest that it might have been his best post-war film. The notes reveal something of a return to the theme of the comradeship of the close-knit creative group (from *Fires were Started*) and a move into a new non-propagandist area for which he felt great sympathy. It looks as if the film would have been basically about the creative 'act of music making' but Jennings' jottings are also full of a feeling for place, humour and above all for the humanity of conductors, musicians, and workmen. There are all sorts of insights and audio-visual ideas in the making: the intercutting at a rehearsal of a conductor's instructions and the comments of the workmen in the roof; 'the cello cases ranged next to ammo boxes and beer crates' at an outside rehearsal; the image from another rehearsal described as 'during the heavenly slow movement the fat and untroubled cleaner mops her way along the stalls'. Not the least revealing parts of the notes are about Vaughan Williams. Jennings admired in him certain qualities which we might ascribe to Jennings – 'his creative fire, and with it his tenacity and above all his humility'. In the same way, his assessment of Vaughan Williams' music is one we could apply to his own war films: he calls *A London Symphony* (music from which Jennings had used in *London Can Take it*) 'not just a piece of great music in the abstract – it is of us, written for us, written about us'.

The music film would have marked a new departure. *Dim Little Island* (1949) returns to national concerns. 'A short film composed on some thoughts about our Past, Present and Future', it examines four facets of national life – temperament, industry, nature and culture. Each facet is given a separate episode in which an expert talks about past and present; then, as the future is discussed, the separate parts are combined and inter-related. Thus, the very construction of the film, aiming to raise morale and inspire confidence in the future, is designed to

114

project national cohesion. The initial mood of the film is set by a shot of rain falling on a puddle (recalling the desperate rain sequence from *A Diary for Timothy*): 'I'chabod, i'chabod, our glory has departed'. The references to the past relate directly to Jennings' view of British history and culture: the extravagant optimism of the Great Exhibition alongside the departing emigrants of 'The Last of England'; the craftsman tradition of shipbuilding and the Depression; the co-existence of nature and industry; the cultural roots of British music in popular folk-song. Both the sentiments and the imagery are less convincing when the film looks into the future. The ideas begin to look conventional. Osbert Lancaster speaks of the British 'remaining deaf to appeals of reason ... convinced that the ex-perts are invariably wrong' while we see shots of a big cargo ship called 'British Genius'. Ian Dalrymple has said that Jennings' discovery of the ship was pure accident − 'but he didn't think it was luck, or coincidence; it was the truth that won't be de-nied'. Nevertheless, accident or not, the effect seems forced and specious, as do the final images of the film, a distant lighthouse flashing, and the faces of the couple from 'The Last of England.' If his 'public imagery' no longer works so fruitfully, it may be because he was trying to impose it on a public which would not recognise and perhaps did not need it, thus making his last films propagandist in a way his war films never were.

In the late 1940s Jennings and Ian Dalrymple had been planning a 'mammoth film ... to commemorate Britain's con-tribution to civilisation in the past hundred years'. They were never able to set this up, but John Grierson offered them the opportunity to make a short film for the Festival of Britain, planned as both a reminiscence and a display of optimism in the future. Bronowski understood from Jennings that in *Family Portrait* 'he wanted to show that the rise of industry a hundred years earlier had been neither smug nor commonplace, but was full of intellectual originality and moral daring'. The film, its images, commentary and music almost entirely organised by Jennings himself, is a personal one in the sense that it is his summing-up of his notions about England, his 'sense of the organic whole of English culture', in Kathleen Raine's phrase.

Formally, *Family Portrait* derives directly from the 1941 shorts and *A Diary for Timothy*, with their love of contrast, association, paradox. It is almost impossible to synopsise since it weaves such a deft web round the history of Britain, reconciling everything to a comprehensible yet complex flow. As one would expect from Jennings, the film is rarely generalised: the names, the places, the locomotives, the processes are specific, yet from them emerges a general spirit. Two threads hold the film together – the ideas of the mixture and confusion of poetry and prose, and of the journey of a nation. In a way a brief encapsulation of the unfinished book, its sense of history is extraordinary. Starting from Beachy Head and the remains of a wartime radar station, recalling the Armada but also the Normans and Romans, the film offers some introductory comments on the diversity of nature and people, evoking Shakespeare. Then the first reference to the mixture of prose and poetry – the silvery moonlit Thames and dark barges and cranes. This introduces Greenwich, Newton, St Paul's – Jennings's 'first stage' – and then coal, Watt, Wilkinson, Trevithick and Stephenson. Suddenly, a dark viaduct and dark waters, grim living and working conditions, but then Blake, Shaftesbury, Dickens and so on. The picture of English history is constantly expanded and enriched by references out to the literature of tolerance, the spirit of enquiry, our origins overseas, our two-way trade with the world. At times Jennings' powers of association and contrast are in full flight: smoke threatens Greenwich but is also the 'emblem of invention' – coal, transport, steel; from Oval cricket ground in the shadow of gas-holders the film moves to trees, Rokhamstead, the hungry forties, Darwin's 'struggle for existence' and commuters on London Bridge; at the Durham Gala we are reminded of Milton's '... not without dust and heat', and the miners' banner is raised by the wind to reveal grey slag heaps beyond; 'shades of the iron masters of old, listen to your hammers stamping the steel discs of the jet age', science and industry – 'which is the poetry, which is the prose?'

Yet despite its undeniable qualities and its centrality to Jennings' thought, *Family Portrait* is finally unsatisfactory. It seems intellectually detached, lacking in passion. The Festival of Britain – very much a non-event – did not provide a forceful enough context for his ideas. The war situation of total threat gave a special intensity to his 'public images'. Here symbols or emblems like Beachy Head, the Long Man of Wilmington or the Oval seem conventional, giving the film a rather remote, institutionalised quality. Similarly the characteristic evening scenes in the war films have an important function, representing a time both of beauty and peace and of maximum danger. The numerous evening shots in *Family Portrait* seem to be chosen less for their suitability than for their mere pictorial qualities. If the film is partly about the journey of a nation, its mood is primarily one of repose, a journey ended.

In *Fires were Started* the only words exchanged about the past are when Johnny Daniels and Barrett ask formally what each did before the war. They joke briefly about it and that is all. It has very little importance for them. The present was too precarious, too precious and vivid, to spend time thinking about the past or, until the later stages of the war (*A Diary for Timothy*) the future. It is no paradox that although people lived only for the present, there was no time when the whole weight of the national past was felt so keenly.

Both *Dim Little Island* and *Family Portrait* refer back explicitly to the past and as if people needed to be reminded of it. Both also seek, however unsuccessfully, to project into the future. *Dim Little Island* especially refers back to the late war as an essential point of departure for the future: the shipyards which moved from depression to wartime activity and back to depression; the nature reserve created from a wartime protected area; the calling up of the spirit of Dunkirk. Most interesting of all is Vaughan Williams on the rebirth of music:

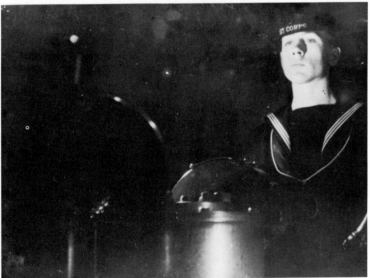

Images of Britain (*Family Portrait*)

The fire is ready to be kindled. Now we require a match to be lighted to set the whole ablaze, some great upheaval of national consciousness and emotion. The Elizabethans experienced this and as a result they produced poetry and music which has never been surpassed. Have we not also lately experienced such a national upheaval?

While he speaks these words, relating directly to Jennings' 1935 essay, we see fire-fighting sequences from *Fires were Started*. The moment tells us much about the source of the passion in Jennings' war films and about what he hoped the upheaval would achieve. Yet the essence of *Dim Little Island* is the admission of disillusion. *Family Portrait* begins and ends with dated snapshots in an album, one of them of the Blitz. And just as in *A Diary for Timothy*, Jennings used Joe Vallance from *Fires were Started* for a sequence of rather melancholy nostalgia, so in *Family Portrait*, in a brief pub scene, he shows B. A. Brown from the same film, still playing the 'comic' but somehow sadly cut off from the war situation in which his life had an immediate validity, both personal and national. It seems symbolic of what had happened to Britain and its individuals. Certainly, while the late films may use the same formal methods and range of reference as the wartime films, they lack a feeling for individuals. Even those people glimpsed only briefly in the war films are given an extraordinary individuality and force. Taken together they constitute a truly national spirit. The late films seem to be prestige productions talking about a nation which is somehow different from the individuals who compose it.

We are told that at the time of his death Jennings' personal optimism remained undimmed. Although this is the view the late films seem to want to project, doubts must remain. The films themselves seek to look forward yet are stated primarily in terms of the past. During the war he sensed and expressed excitement, purpose, fulfilment. *A Diary for Timothy* already looked forward with apprehension to a peace that would endanger this mood. The post-war films try to continue the wartime mood but his sensibility, despite himself, looked back

Family Portrait

rather than forward. His last paintings appear to have reverted to a series on the Plough and the Windmill. Kathleen Raine recalls Jennings at this time surveying the industrial landscape of Battersea and saying: 'This has all grown up within less than two hundred years. Has anyone ever suggested that this is the way in which human beings ought to live? It will all have to go, it has been a terrible mistake!' These are not thoughts, one feels, that would have come to him in wartime. Under the surface of the last films is an edge of desperation. Perhaps consciously or unconsciously, he lacked a new vision, confidence in the future. And perhaps the world he looked at lacked it too.

Filmography

Humphrey Jennings

1907   Born in Walberswick, Suffolk, and then educated at Perse School and Pembroke College, Cambridge, where he read English. After taking his degree he remained in Cambridge, doing post-graduate research, painting and writing poetry. He also designed for the Cambridge Repertory Theatre, and was connected with Mass Observation.

1934   Began working with the GPO Film Unit, first on scenic design, taking small acting parts in *Pett and Pott* and *Glorious Sixth of June*, and editing compilation films.

1936   Went to work on Shell Films with Len Lye.

1938   Came back to the GPO Film Unit; he directed documentary films for them (as the Crown Film Unit) throughout and after the war. There was an exhibition of his paintings in the same year.

1949   Started to direct for Wessex Films, and was commissioned to make *Family Portrait* (1950) as one of the official films for the Festival of Britain.

1950   Left England for Greece to make *The Good Life*, a film to be one of a series to be called *The Changing Face of Europe*. While working on the island of Poros, he died as the result of a fall from a cliff.

Jennings played the part of a telegraph boy in *Glorious Sixth of June* and appeared as a grocer in *Pett and Pott*, both directed by Cavalcanti in 1934.

Films on which Jennings worked
Post-Haste (1934)

Production company	GPO Film Unit
Editor	Humphrey Jennings

Running time: 26 min
Copy held in National Film Archive

Pett and Pott (1934)

Production company	GPO Film Unit
Producer	John Grierson
Director	Cavalcanti
Photography	John Taylor
Sets	Humphrey Jennings

Running time: 33 min
Distributor: British Film Institute

The Story of the Wheel (1934)

Production company	GPO Film Unit
Editor	Humphrey Jennings

Photographed from models and diagrams in the British Museum, London Museum, and Science Museum
Running time: 12 min
Copy held in National Film Archive

Locomotives (1935)

Production company	GPO Film Unit
Editor	Humphrey Jennings

| Music | Ballet music from Schubert's 'Rosamunde', arranged by John Foulds |

Photographed from models in the Science Museum, South Kensington
Running time: 21 min
Copy held in National Film Archive

The Birth of a Robot (1936)

Production company	Shell Oil Company
Producer	Len Lye
Director	Len Lye
Script	C. H. David
Photography	Alex Strasser
Colour direction and production	Humphrey Jennings
Colour process	Gasparcolour
Design and construction of models	John Banting, Alan Fanner
Sound recording	Jack Ellitt
Music	Holst, Planets Suite

Running time: 7 min
Distributor: British Film Institute

Penny Journey (1938)

Production company	GPO Film Unit
Director	Humphrey Jennings
Photography	Henry Fowle, W. B. Pollard

Running time: 6 min
Copy held in National Film Archive

123

Spare Time (1939)

Production company	GPO Film Unit
Producer	Cavalcanti
Director/Script	Humphrey Jennings
Commentary	Laurie Lee
Photography	Henry Fowle
Music	Played by the Steel, Peach and Tozer Phoenix Works Band, the Manchester Victorian Carnival Band, and the Handel Male Voice Choir
Sound recording	Yorke Scarlett

Running time: 18 min
Copy held in National Film Archive

Speaking from America (1939)

Production company	GPO Film Unit
Director	Humphrey Jennings
Photography	W. B. Pollard, F. Gamage
Diagrams	J. Chambers
Commentary	R. Duff
Sound recording	Ken Cameron

Running time: 10 min
Copy held in National Film Archive

SS Ionian (*Her Last Trip*) (1939)

Production company	GPO Film Unit
Director	Humphrey Jennings

Running time: 20 min
Copy held in National Film Archive
Cargoes (9 min approx) was a shorter version of this film

124

The First Days (1939) originally *A City Prepares*

Production company	GPO Film Unit
Producer	Cavalcanti
Directors	Humphrey Jennings, Harry Watt, Pat Jackson
Commentary	Robert Sinclair
Editor	R. Q. McNaughton

Running time: 23 min
Copy held in National Film Archive

London Can Take It (1940)

Production company	GPO Film Unit, for the Ministry of Information
Directors	Humphrey Jennings, Harry Watt
Photography	Henry Fowle, Jonah Jones
Music	Vaughan Williams 'A London Symphony'
Commentary	Quentin Reynolds
Sound recording	R. A. Cameron

Running time: 10 min
Distributor: British Film Institute
London Can Take It was intended primarily for export to North and South
America. A five minute version for the domestic market, *Britain Can Take
It*, was adapted from it

Spring Offensive (1940), theatrical title *An Unrecorded Victory*

Production company	GPO Film Unit, for the Ministry of Information
Producer	Cavalcanti
Director	Humphrey Jennings
Script	Hugh Gray
Commentary	A. G. Street
Photography	Henry Fowle, Jonah Jones, Eric Gross
Editor	Geoff Foot
Artistic director	Edward Carrick

Music	Liszt, arranged by Brian Easdale and conducted by Muir Mathieson
Sound recording	Ken Cameron

Running time: 20 min
Copy held in National Film Archive

Welfare of the Workers (1940)

Production company	GPO Film Unit, for the Ministry of Information
Producer	Harry Watt
Assistant producer	J. B. Holmes
Director	Humphrey Jennings, P. Jackson
Photography	Jonah Jones
Editor	Jack Lee
Commentary	Ritchie Calder
Sound recording	Ken Cameron

Running time: 10 min
Copy held in National Film Archive

Heart of Britain (1941)

Production company	Crown Film Unit, for the Ministry of Information
Producer	Ian Dalrymple
Director	Humphrey Jennings
Photography	Henry Fowle
Editor	Stewart McAllister
Music	Beethoven and Handel, played by the Hallé Orchestra conducted by Sir Malcolm Sergeant; and the Huddersfield Choir
Commentary	Jack Holmes
Sound	Ken Cameron

A slightly longer version, *This is England*, with a commentary by Ed Murrow, was made for export to North and South America.
Running time: 9 min
Copy held in National Film Archive

Words for Battle (1941)

Production company	Crown Film Unit for Ministry of Information
Producer	Ian Dalrymple
Director/Script	Humphrey Jennings
Editor	Stewart McAllister
Music	Beethoven and Handel, played by the London Philharmonic Orchestra conducted by Sir Malcolm Sargeant
Sound recording	Ken Cameron
Commentary	Laurence Olivier

Running time: 8 min
Distributor: British Film Institute/Central Film Library

Listen to Britain (1942)

Production company	Crown Film Unit, for Ministry of Information
Producer	Ian Dalrymple
Director/Script/Editor	Humphrey Jennings, Stewart McAllister
Assistant director	Joe Mendoza
Photography	Henry Fowle
Foreword spoken by	Leonard Brockington
Sound recording	Ken Cameron

Running time: 20 min
Distributor: British Film Institute/Central Film Library

Fires Were Started (left); and Jennings with Dame Myra Hess during the shooting of *A Diary for Timothy*

Fires were Started (*I Was a Fireman*) (1943)

Production company	Crown Film Unit, with the co-operation of the Home Office, Ministry of Home Security, and National Fire Service
Producer	Ian Dalrymple
Director/Script	Humphrey Jennings
Story collaboration	Maurice Richardson
Photography	C. Pennington-Richards
Sets	Edward Carrick
Editor	Stewart McAllister
Music	William Alwyn, directed by Muir Mathieson
Sound recording	Ken Cameron, Jock May

C. Officer George Gravett (*Sub-Officer Dykes*), Lt. Fireman Philip Dickson (*Fireman Walters*), Lt. Fireman Fred Griffiths (*Johnny Daniels*), Lt. Fireman Loris Rey (*J. Rumbold*), Fireman Johnny Houghton (*S. H. Jackson*), Fireman T. P. Smith (*B. A. Brown*), Fireman John Barker (*J.

Vallance), Fireman W. Sansom (*Barrett*), Asst. Group Officer Green (Mrs. Townsend), Firewoman Betty Martin (*Betty*), Firewoman Eileen White (*Eileen*).

Running time: 80 min
Distributor: British Film Institute

The Silent Village (1943)

Production company	Crown Film Unit, for Ministry of Information
Producer/Director/Script	Humphrey Jennings
Assistant director	Diana Pine
Photography	Henry Fowle
Editor	Stewart McAllister
Sound	Jock May
Music	Title and incidental music specially composed by Beckitt Williams, orchestra conducted by Muir Mathieson. Welsh songs sung by Morriston United Male Choir, and hymns by Cwmgiedd Chapel Congregation

Running time: 36 min
Distributor: Central Film Library

The Eighty Days (1944)

Production company	Crown Film Unit, for Ministry of Information
Producer/Director	Humphrey Jennings
Commentary	Ed Murrow

Running time: 14 min
Distributor: Central Film Library

The True Story of Lilli Marlene (1944)

Production company	Crown Film Unit
Producer	J. B. Holmes
Director	Humphrey Jennings
Assistant director	Graham Wallace
Script	Humphrey Jennings
Photography	Henry Fowle
Sets	Edward Carrick
Editor	Sid Stone
Music	Denis Blood, directed by Muir Mathieson

Running time: 30 min
Copy held in National Film Archive

*V*1 (1944)

Production company	Crown Film Unit
Producer	Humphrey Jennings
Commentary	Fletcher Markle

Made for overseas use only
Running time: 10 min
Copy held in National Film Archive

A Diary for Timothy (1944–5)

Production company	Crown Film Unit
Producer	Basil Wright
Director/Script	Humphrey Jennings
Commentary written by	E. M. Forster
Commentary spoken by	Michael Redgrave
Photography	Fred Gamage
Editor	Alan Osbiston, Jenny Hutt

Music	Richard Addinsell, played by the London Symphony Orchestra conducted by Muir Mathieson
Sound recording	Ken Cameron, Jock May

Running time: 39 min
Distributor: British Film Institute

A Defeated People (1946)

Production company	Crown Film Unit, for Directorate of Army Kinematography with the co-operation of the Allied Control Commission of Germany, and of the Army Film Unit
Producer	Basil Wright
Director/Script	Humphrey Jennings
Photography	Army Film Unit
Music	Guy Warwick, played by London Symphony Orchestra conducted by Muir Mathieson
Commentary spoken by	William Hartnell

Running time: 19 min
Copy held in National Film Archive

The Cumberland Story (1947)

Production company	Crown Film Unit for the Central Office of Information, for the Ministry of Fuel and Power with the co-operation of the United Steel Companies and the National Union of Mineworkers
Producer	Alexander Shaw
Director/Script	Humphrey Jennings
Photography	Henry Fowle
Art director	Scott MacGregor, John Cooper
Editor	Jocelyn Jackson

131

Music   Arthur Benjamin, played by the Philharmonic
                             Orchestra conducted by Muir Mathieson
Sound recording   Jock May

Running time: 39 min
Copy held in National Film Archive

Dim Little Island (1949)

Production company   Wessex Films for the Central Office of
                             Information
Producer/Director   Humphrey Jennings
Photography   Martin Curtis
Editor   Bill Megarry
Music   Ralph Vaughan Williams
Commentary   Osbert Lancaster, John Ormston, James Fisher,
                             Ralph Vaughan Williams

Running time: 11 min
Distributor: British Film Institute

Family Portrait (1950)

Production company   Wessex Films
Producer   Ian Dalrymple
Director/Script   Humphrey Jennings
Assistant director   Harley Usill
Photography   Martin Curtis
Editor   Stewart McAllister
Music   John Greenwood, orchestra conducted by Muir
                             Mathieson
Commentary   Michael Goodliffe
Sound recording   Ken Cameron

Made for the Festival of Britain
Running time: 25 min
Distributor: Central Film Library

132

3: Free Cinema

If Free Cinema were compared with the Documentary movement of the 1930s, it would undoubtedly come off worse. The Documentary movement of the thirties lasted longer, produced more, was more sustained, more ambitious than Free Cinema. It created a sponsorship structure for the documentary film that became a permanent part of the British Cinema and also had important effects on the documentary production system in other countries. Free Cinema's experiments in sponsorship were confined to making use of the British Film Institute's Experimental Fund, which had come into existence independently of Free Cinema, and to a short-lived experiment with the Ford Motor Company. Lastly, the critical discussion of the cinema promoted by Grierson and his associates ranged further and deeper.

But the comparison isn't quite legitimate. In talking about the Documentary movement of the thirties we are talking about something more or less *complete*, an activity which involved Grierson, Wright, Rotha, Elton, Anstey and others totally for a major part of their careers. In talking about Free Cinema we are talking about something *partial*, an activity which is best regarded as an episode in the development of a particular tendency within the British cinema. To make the comparison a fairer one, Free Cinema must be put together with the critical magazines, *Sequence* and the *Sight and Sound* of the period 1950–58, and the careers as feature film-makers (which are, of course, far from over) of Lindsay Anderson, Karel Reisz and Tony Richardson. The point of such a comparison is to draw attention to the position of intellectuals in the British cinema. On the face of it, from the 1930s to the present intellectuals seem to have been intimately connected with the documentary film. In the 1930s, young intellectuals expressed themselves completely through the documentary film. If Free Cinema is considered in isolation, the succeeding generation of intellectuals appears to have worked in the same way; but if it is related to *Sequence*, and to feature films like *Saturday Night and Sunday Morning*, *A Taste of Honey*, *This Sporting Life*, *Isadora*, *The Sailor from Gibraltar* and *If . . .*, the continuity is not so apparent. The development of the generation which succeeded the documentarists of the thirties has had something of a different character, which has changed the focus of interest in the British cinema away from the documentary film.

Background ideas

Though Free Cinema was only an episode in the development of a tendency, it still provides a convenient vantage point for examining that tendency. Concretely, Free Cinema consisted of six programmes of films presented at the National Film Theatre between 1956 and 1959. These programmes were:

1. *O Dreamland* (directed by Lindsay Anderson), *Momma Don't Allow* (Tony Richardson and Karel Reisz), *Together* (Lorenza Mazzetti and Denis Horne) – shown February 1956.

2. *Neighbours* (Norman McLaren), *Le Sang des Bêtes* (Georges Franju), *On the Bowery* (Lionel Rogosin) – shown September 1956.

3. *The Singing Street* (N. Isaac, J. Ritchie and R. Townsend), *Wakefield Express* (Lindsay Anderson), *Nice Time* (Alain Tanner and Claude Goretta), *Every Day Except Christmas* (Lindsay Anderson) – shown May 1957 under the general title *Look at Britain*.

4. *Where the Devil Says Goodnight* (K. Karabasz and W. Slesicki), *Paragraph Zero* (W. Borowik), *Island of Great Hope* (B. Poreba), *The House of Old Women* (J. Lomnicki), *Once upon a Time* (Jan Lenica and Walerian Borowczyk), *Dom* (Jan Lenica and Walerian Borowczyk), *Two Men and a Wardrobe* (R. Polanski) – shown September 1958 under the general title *Polish Voices.*

5. *Les Mistons* (François Truffaut), *Le Beau Serge* (Claude Chabrol) – shown September 1958 under the general title *French Renewal.*

6. *Food for a Blush* (Elizabeth Russell), *Enginemen* (Michael Grigsby), *Refuge England* (Robert Vas), *We are the Lambeth Boys* (Karel Reisz) – shown March 1959 under the general title *The Last Free Cinema.*

The people responsible for the presentation of these programmes were an informal group, the most active of whom were Lindsay Anderson, who at this time was best known as a critic but who had already made a number of documentary films; Karel Reisz, who had been programme planner of the National Film Theatre as well as writing criticism, but was now turning to documentary film-making; John Fletcher, a documentary film-maker who was something of a technical jack-of-all-trades; and the documentary cameraman Walter Lassally. On occasion they were identified as the Committee for Free Cinema.

In the broadest terms, Free Cinema had two objectives: to show what it valued in the cinema, with the emphasis on the work of young contemporary film-makers; and by showing films to encourage other films to be made. The ideas behind the presentation of the programmes were stated most directly in the written material that accompanied them. As this material was usually a cross between a manifesto and a press hand-out, the ideas are not stated precisely. To understand them fully, reference needs to be made to the articles about Free Cinema which Anderson and Reisz contributed to *Universities and Left Review* (which also organised showings of the Free Cinema films in towns outside London), and to some of the general pieces written by Anderson at the time: notably 'Stand Up! Stand Up!' in *Sight and Sound* and 'Get out and Push' in the book *Declaration*.

From these sources, three main ideas can be discerned: one, freedom for the film-maker; two, the film-maker as a commentator on contemporary society; three, the necessity for 'commitment' on the part of the film-maker and the critic.

As the movement's title suggests, freedom for the film-maker was the central idea. 'Freedom' in this context means two different but related things. First, it was identified as the film-maker's ability to express himself personally through his films. 'THESE FILMS ARE FREE in the sense that their statements are entirely personal,' said one of Free Cinema's first hand-outs, and 'No film can be too personal'. In its second meaning it referred to the film-maker's freedom from the restraints imposed by commercial systems of film-making. The same hand-out said, 'Most of them [the films], so far, have been produced outside the framework of the film industry. This has meant that their directors have been able to express their own viewpoints, sometimes unusual, without obligation to subscribe to the technical or social conventions imposed on work under commercial conditions.'

All Free Cinema propaganda showed a concern with the relationship between art and society. As it was presented by Free Cinema, the nature of this relationship was taken for granted. The film-maker should be a commentator on contemporary society: one of the qualities claimed for the British films shown in the programmes was the fact that they portrayed contemporary society. 'Candid exploration of contemporary Britain has been an important part of this tradition,' said a statement accompanying the last Free Cinema programme.

This insistence that a direct relationship between the film-maker and society was valuable seems to have been based on two assumptions: that the portrayal of contemporary society was an essential function of the documentary film, and that art

136

which did not have a direct relationship with society was likely to become trivial and insipid. Much emphasis was put on this second assumption. In 'Get out and Push', Anderson argued:

'Britain must be one of the few countries in the world where artists insist on confining themselves to the manufacture of entertainment (more or less high-class) or to onanism, and lash out in angry fear when anybody suggests that their range might be extended if they could relate their work to the world outside themselves, or at least consider their art in relation to their fellow-men.'

An insistence on a close relationship between art and society seems to lead on naturally to the idea of commitment on the part of the artist. In fact, 'art and society' and 'commitment' were treated as separate themes in most of Free Cinema writing, and no attempt was made to link them as part of a systematic position. The necessity for 'commitment' on the part of the artist may suggest an idea like Sartre's 'engagement'. But, in fact, it had much more in common with British non-conformist ideas than with Sartre, as the title of Anderson's essay 'Stand Up! Stand Up!' indicates. This essay and 'Get out and Push' both argue that an artist or critic unavoidably has values which he expresses in his work, and that he should have the courage to be explicit about these values and to fight for them. Anderson took it for granted that the values were liberal, humanist ones. The last sentences of 'Get out and Push' neatly sum up his notion of 'commitment': 'But one thing is certain: in the values of humanism, and in their determined application to our society, lies the future. All we have to do is to believe in them.'

These ideas were not developed in any theoretical way, even in the longer and more sustained articles. The characteristic method was to develop them through attacks on the established film industry, both feature and documentary. In his article on Free Cinema in *Universities and Left Review*, Karel Reisz developed the ideas of freedom for the film-maker and the film-maker's relationship with society by way of an attack on an example of prestige documentary film-making, *Song of the*

Clouds. He began by criticising the lack of any personal quality in the film:

Song of the Clouds has some distinguished names on its credits and, the scientific film apart, represents the norm of our documentary industry. From the film-maker's point of view this is particularly disturbing because the film represents the almost complete abdication of the creator of the film, the director. A film of this kind is planned in terms of the facts it will have to present; it is conceived in committee; it has a commentary written by another hand, which tries to give the images a weight they do not have. Under these conditions, the director's function becomes that of a technician.

Going on to discuss the relationship between the film-maker and society, Reisz argued that the documentary film now had little contact with contemporary life, and that the established documentary film-makers had changed sides:

Where in the 30s they made valuable films about life as it was lived in this country ... today they make at best the (admittedly valuable) scientific film or, at worst, spend their time 'projecting Britain' (this means films about the Lake District, Stirling Moss, old trams, and the beauties of spring).

Similar charges were made against the feature film industry. In 'Get out and Push', Lindsay Anderson characterised the British feature film as snobbish and class-bound. He also attacked it for the archaic image of Britain it presented and for its evasion of contemporary reality.

The film industry wasn't the only target. Free Cinema's ideas were also stated by way of an assault on liberal culture. Anderson in particular developed the ideas of the relationship between the artist and society and the need for 'commitment' through critical analyses of existing liberal culture, which for him was represented by the *New Statesman*, the *Observer*, the writers like Kingsley Amis and John Wain. He diagnosed the weaknesses of this culture as the separation of art from society so that art was seen as a diversion and entertainment only, and embarrassment and boredom with the liberal values it was supposed to stand for.

The films

In examining the films presented in the Free Cinema pro-grammes, it seems sensible to concentrate on the British films since they formed the most coherent part of the programmes. They were the work of people who were in close touch with each other, who were in a position to see and discuss each others' films. The foreign films were made in different cultural contexts, and by people whose association with the Free Cinema film-makers was either remote or non-existent. This is not to say that the foreign films had no proper place in the programmes. They were all good illustrations of Free Cinema's demand for freedom of expression and a personal point of view on the part of the artist. The choice of foreign films revealed a great sensitivity to new artists, since it included early films from Franju, Truffaut, Chabrol, Lenica, Borowczyk and Polanski, all of whom were unknown at that time. In retrospect the grouping of these films with the English ones can be seen as the first signs of what later came to be known as the 'new wave', the emergence of a significant number of new young directors in the film industries of most European countries (most obviously in France).

How did the British films relate to Free Cinema's general ideas? In the first place, how good examples were they of *free* cinema? If freedom is interpreted as meaning freedom from the restraints and conventions imposed by commercial structures, the Free Cinema films were undoubtedly successful. None of them looks like the conventional documentaries of the time. Their subjects are different: the jazz-club of *Momma Don't Allow* and the young people and service-men at a loose end of *Nice Time* were not the kind of subjects dealt with in the established documentaries. There is a freshness and intimacy in the observation, a willingness on the part of the film-makers to respond directly to what they see. Films like *Momma Don't*

Allow and *We are the Lambeth Boys* view young people without any of the distortingly crude pre-conceptions about them that were current in public discussion at that time. All the films have some of the qualities of the very earliest documentaries, where the camera's ability to capture the world about it surprises and charms the spectator.

If freedom is interpreted as the expressing of a personal point of view, only two films, *O Dreamland* and *Together*, have claims to consideration. *O Dreamland* is a reportage of a seaside funfair. Shots of the amusements offered and of people amusing themselves are made into a critical comment on the funfair by the juxtaposition of shots with each other and with the soundtrack. An adverse response to this kind of entertainment is not particularly novel; the film's personal quality arises not from its point of view but out of the disproportion between the feeling generated and the subject that generates the feeling. The intense exasperation revealed isn't easy to justify. In this respect, *O Dreamland* can usefully be compared with *A propos de Nice*. Like Anderson, Vigo roots his film in the observation of a particular place. He also responds intensely to his subject. But in *A propos de Nice* there is a proportion between response and observation. Vigo's anger is justified by his presentation of Nice as the epitome of decaying bourgeois society. In *O Dreamland* the funfair never gains any representative quality. The essential difference between the two films is the surrealism which encourages Vigo to go beyond direct reportage.

Together, with its fictional element and its refined means of expression (long takes, formal composition, slow editing rhythms), is very different from the rest of the Free Cinema films. The only characteristics it has in common with them are a documentary setting and a working-class background. But in its portrait of two closed worlds – that of the deaf mutes and that of a traditional working-class community – and in the way it relates one world to the other, so that the deaf mutes experience a familiar, everyday world as hostile and menacing, it expresses a personal vision.

140

Nice Time (above); *We Are the Lambeth Boys* (centre); *Together*

Apart from these two films, the views of the world which emerge from Free Cinema films are recognisable, the result of preoccupations common among intellectuals in the second half of the 1950s. Broadly, these preoccupations were: a sympathetic interest in communities, whether they were the traditional industrial one of *Wakefield Express* or the new, improvised one of the jazz club in *Momma Don't Allow*; fascination with the newly emerging youth culture (*Momma Don't Allow*, *We are the Lambeth Boys*, *Nice Time*); unease about the quality of leisure in an urban society (*Nice Time* and *O Dreamland*); and respect for the traditional working class (*Enginemen* and *Every Day except Christmas*).

It is obvious from what has already been said about the films that almost all reflected the idea that the film-maker should be directly involved with contemporary society. With the possible exceptions of *Together* and *Food for a Blush*, all could be described as portraits of British society in the 1950s. Like *Look back in Anger* in the theatre, part of their impact on audiences came from the representation of the contemporary world on the screen, where before it had been firmly ignored.

The involvement of the film-maker with contemporary society seems a perfectly appropriate idea in view of the kind of films that the Free Cinema film-makers produced. The idea of commitment, on the other hand, doesn't seem to have a particular relevance. It might be possible to argue that the films revealed a commitment to liberal, humanist values. But this commitment hardly had a decisive effect on the character of the films. If the idea of commitment is looked at in terms of individual films it is only relevant to *O Dreamland*, which was the only film to have an aggressive polemical quality that matched Anderson's call to artists and critics to be ready to fight for their values. But how accurate is it to claim that *O Dreamland* expresses liberal, humanist values? My own view is that the film shows two attitudes which are not necessarily related. There is the criticism of the shoddiness of the entertainment offered by the funfair, which might be seen as coming from liberal, humanist sentiments. And there is distaste for physical appearances (large bottoms, baggy clothes) by which the adults (except for occasional old people) are contrasted with children; it is hard to see how this could be called an expression of liberal, humanist values.

Free Cinema aesthetics

Free Cinema didn't show any great interest in aesthetic problems. Its aesthetic attitudes were expressed in a gnomic fashion in a statement accompanying the first programme: 'The image speaks. Sound amplifies and comments. Size is irrelevant. Perfection is not an aim. An attitude means a style. A style means an attitude'. In so far as these claims are not truisms, they indicate suspicion of the commercial film because of the emphasis put on technical perfection and technical development. ('Size is irrelevant' presumably refers to CinemaScope and allied developments which were then coming into use.) And if we were to accept the claim 'An attitude means a style. A style means an attitude', the important question of style in the cinema would be very simply resolved.

Free Cinema's aesthetic attitude is best examined by looking at the films. Reportage is the basic method. Apart from *Together*, every one of the films could be described as a reportage. In this area the Free Cinema film-makers took advantage of new technical developments: lighter and more flexible equipment, and faster film stock. By making use of these new developments, the film-makers were able to give their reportages an intimacy and vividness new to the documentary cinema. *Nice Time* is the most striking example of these qualities. Without the freedom the new developments gave, its candid camera view of Piccadilly Circus would have been enormously inhibited. Flexibility and willingness to take chances on the part of Free Cinema technicians, particularly John Fletcher and Walter Lassally, were very important to success in this whole area. But the outstanding achievement so far as the reportage was concerned was *We are the Lambeth Boys*. Taking advantage of the

143

new flexibility, Karel Reisz was able to refine the quality of his observation of the youth club which is the centre of the film. Whereas in the traditional documentary film the observer's position was obviously external, Reisz was able to move in close to his subject so that his position became more that of a participant, involved but with a certain detachment. Especially important to this achievement was the use of sound. The microphone listens to the young people talking just as sensitively as the camera observes them dancing, playing cricket or at work.

The Free Cinema film-makers wanted their films to be more than reportages. Attempts were made to add extra dimensions of meaning to the observation of a subject so that the films were commentaries on it as well as reports of it. The aesthetic means used to do this were: montage techniques (*Nice Time*, for example, works on the Eisensteinian principle of cutting two shots together so that their juxtaposition suggests some general meaning more than the individual shots contain in themselves); sound-image disjunctions (a very typical example is provided by *O Dreamland* where the mechanical laughter of a dummy carries on over unrelated images so that the whole funfair comes to have a manic quality); commentary (used as a direct carrier of meaning, particularly in *Every Day except Christmas* and *We are the Lambeth Boys*); and simple dramatisation (*Refuge England* was built around the situation of a refugee wandering through London looking for a vague address he had been given).

Free Cinema as a Movement

Free Cinema's general ideas were hardly novel. The demand for a cinema that does not impose restraints on the artist's self-expression has been a persistent plea throughout the cinema's history. The call for a cinema to portray contemporary society has also been made several times before, notably by the British documentarists of the thirties and the Italian Neo-realists.

Nor do the ideas constitute a particularly coherent position. For example, the artist's right to self-expression contradicts the demand that films should portray contemporary society. If the

144

film-maker's right to self-expression is absolute, he can't also be told that his films should concentrate on a particular kind of subject matter.

Similarly, Free Cinema's aesthetic methods are long-established ones. To give some random examples: Vigo had used the same principle of editing that Goretta and Tanner used in *Nice Time*, and Anderson used in *O Dreamland*; Jennings had used sound-image disjunctions in most of his films; dramatisation was the usual method of British documentarists – Harry Watt, for example. Indeed, in their use of commentary the British Free Cinema films were very conventional: films like *Every Day except Christmas* and *We are the Lambeth Boys* seem to have learnt nothing from one of the foreign films shown in the second Free Cinema programme – *Le Sang des Bêtes*. In both the British documentaries, the commentary remains outside the dramatic structure of the film and does little but provide background information and comment. In *Le Sang des Bêtes* Franju, by using two contrasting voices and giving them different functions, took the commentary inside the dramatic framework of his film and made it an integral part.

Looked at as a movement like Neo-realism or the Soviet cinema of the twenties, Free Cinema seems minor and limited, a dwarf movement. But perhaps this is the wrong perspective to use. In interviews in *Cinema International* in 1967, both Lindsay Anderson and Karel Reisz argued that Free Cinema wasn't really a movement. Anderson said: 'Free Cinema wasn't part of an intellectual movement. If you're trying to describe its meaning in this country, the key word is *empirical*. Free Cinema came into existence for essentially practical reasons.' Reisz added: 'We made films and wrote manifestos to provide a little publicity for the movement, but the value of these films, if they have one, lies in the films themselves and not in the movement.'

Should Free Cinema's appearance as a movement be regarded simply as a disguise? Would it be better viewed as the effort of a group of young film-makers to gain a place in the film industry? In fact one of the more important objectives of any movement has usually been the replacing of established figures by new, not yet established artists. That this should have been one of Free Cinema's aims does not disqualify it from being a movement. The essential question is whether Free Cinema had any other objectives besides this one.

The answer to this is undoubtedly, yes. The ideas Free Cinema expressed were more than useful improvisations for publicity purposes. They were in line with the attitudes developed over a number of years by Free Cinema spokesmen in their critical writing in *Sequence* and *Sight and Sound*. I've already suggested that Free Cinema was part of something larger. If it is related to its origins in *Sequence* and *Sight and Sound*, the ideas it expressed can be seen as the outcome of an attempt to formulate a general position on the cinema.

Sequence

Sequence was firstly the magazine of the Oxford University Film Society; later it became an independent journal published in London. In all fourteen issues were published, between 1947 and 1952. Even before *Sequence* stopped appearing, some of its contributors became involved with the British Film Institute's magazine, *Sight and Sound*. Gavin Lambert, one of Sequence's editors, became editor of *Sight and Sound* in 1950.

Though *Sequence* was rarely explicit about its basic principles, a general view of the cinema is easy to deduce from its writings. The best indication of this view was given in a valedictory article by Gavin Lambert. He picked out a key sentence from the second issue: 'In the cinema the spirit of delight comes less frequently than in any other art.' 'As it turned out,' he went on, 'during the next four years the spirit of delight came more frequently than one might have expected.'* Lambert took it for

---

* It is worth mentioning that this happened because the cinema of the late 1940s was a special case. The post-war boom in audiences meant that the level of production was high. Added to this a large number of films which had not reached Britain because of the war began to be shown.

Nice Time (left); and *Refuge England*

granted that the main purpose of art was to give pleasure. He also suggested that the recognition of the success of a particular film in giving pleasure wasn't difficult. 'In the first place, one responds – to a style, to a vision, an alert observation, to something that engages the imagination or the senses or (rarely in the cinema) the intellect. To respond, to be aware that one is responding is simple enough. Basically, it is telling the difference between being bored and not being bored.'

This was the basis of *Sequence*'s critical aesthetic, to respond directly and immediately to a film. It was only a little more specific about what the critic responded to. The quality most frequently referred to in the magazine was 'poetry', by its very nature difficult to define. In his article 'Creative Elements', Lindsay Anderson gave the best exposition of the group's critical aesthetic:

Style and content fuse to form something new, something individual, a whole greater than its parts. A synopsis of *L'Atalante* means as little as one of a lyric poem; on paper *My Darling Clementine* is just another Western. But as they unfold upon the screen, with grace of movement, freshness of vision, they are found to possess a magic power to excite, to enchant, to revive. To describe this as 'formal beauty' is inadequate and misleading, for the phrase implies the frigid, sterile formality of a work like *Day of Wrath*, rather than the living poetry which is the result even when a commonplace story is given shape and meaning by an expressive camera, sympathetic music and design, skilled actors, and above all by creative direction which gathers all these elements together and gives them unity and life.

As the last sentence of this quotation makes clear, *Sequence* had little doubt that the creative responsibility for a film was one man's, the director's. Anderson argued this point very specifically in his article 'The Director's Cinema'. Even more indicative of *Sequence*'s belief in the supremacy of the director was its practical criticism. The centrepiece of almost every issue was a long and careful analysis of a director's work; articles were published on the work of Ford, Preston Sturges, Wyler, Hitchcock, Cocteau, Carné, Donskoi, Clair, Disney and Arne Sucksdorff.

Even though this belief in the director was firmly held, it was based on pragmatic rather than theoretical grounds. *Sequence* took account of the work of a cameraman like Gregg Toland, or a writer like Dudley Nichols. Gavin Lambert described the pragmatic way the belief was arrived at: 'You discover in nearly all the most impressive films it is the director who creates the fusion of all these talents, and you note the others erratically if they happen to be outstandingly good or bad.'

The belief that quality in the cinema came from one man's ability to express himself naturally led *Sequence* to a hostility to the commercial framework of the film industry. This hostility was taken for granted and not examined; as a result, the contradiction between large numbers of the films *Sequence* valued, most of which had been made within the orthodox commercial framework, and the supposed evil influence of the framework, was never recognised.

From this description of *Sequence*'s basic principles it should be obvious that Free Cinema in important respects grew directly from *Sequence*: art as personal expression; 'poetry' as the supreme quality of a film; the director as the artist; hostility to the commercial structure – all these ideas were common to *Sequence* and Free Cinema.

Free Cinema was anticipated by *Sequence* in even more specific ways. In an article criticising the limitations imposed on film-makers working within orthodox commercial structures, Lindsay Anderson suggested that the only possible alternative was independent small-scale production. He identified this kind of film-making with the creation of an avant-garde, by which, he was careful to add, he did not mean only experimental, surrealist-type films. Having listed a number of films which he thought belonged in this broad avant-garde category (British documentary films of the 1930s, Roy Kellino's *I Met a Murderer*, Vigo's films, and Benoît-Levy's *La Maternelle* among others), he went on to describe the films in terms he might equally well have applied to the Free Cinema films:

Their limitations are obvious: they lack polish, film stock is often bad, lighting variable, sets (where used) unconvincing. Yet they date less, or less damagingly than more elaborate productions because they have not compromised with the fashions and prejudices of their time; execution has followed from conception, not from the demands of box office. They remain fresh, spontaneous, individual.

Even more specifically, discussing some recent American and Canadian shorts in an article called 'Free Cinema', Alan Cooke wrote:

I prefer to group these films under another heading – Free Cinema – which has the advantage of being inclusive rather than exclusive, of

149

indicating a genre to which we may credit all films which please or illuminate without compromise or self-mutilation. *Muscle Beach* is an example of Free Cinema, and so is *Fireworks*. So (amongst the films discussed elsewhere in this issue) are *Wagonmaster*, *Les Dames du Bois de Bologne*, *Orphée*. All these films, however diverse their intentions, have one achievement in common: an expressive and personal use of the medium. Free Cinema includes the acknowledged successes as well as the films *maudits*, the traditionalist as well as the experimentalist; it constitutes the real avant-garde, the true aristocracy of the cinema.

(In Elizabeth Sussex's book about Lindsay Anderson, Anderson is reported as saying, 'I had rewritten this article to make it a bit more "important". I coined the phrase "Free Cinema" which I put into the last paragraph, and I called the article "Free Cinema".')

These quotations help us to consider Free Cinema's peculiar character when looked on as a movement. Free Cinema was modelled on avant-garde movements like Surrealism; but the idea of 'Free' was inimical to the basic character of such movements. It was a very broad notion (a 'free' film was more or less any film the critic responded to) that allowed many different films to be grouped together. So, though Free Cinema was presented as a movement, it lacked one of the essential characteristics of a movement, a clear definition of itself.

Differences between Free Cinema and Sequence

The continuity between Free Cinema and *Sequence* was not perfect. Free Cinema had certain characteristics foreign to *Sequence*, which could broadly be described under the heading of social involvement. *Sequence* concentrated on art as an independent phenomenon, not showing much concern with its relationship to other social phenomena. The involvement with the documentary film, the emphasis on the film's relationship to contemporary society and the idea of commitment, are not to be found in *Sequence*; while not directly hostile to the documentary, *Sequence* showed little interest in it as a specific form of cinema. Certain documentary directors were admired – Jennings, Flaherty, Sucksdorff – but not specifically because they made documentaries. The British documentary cinema, still at that time a lively if increasingly frustrated force, was generally ignored. Where it was mentioned it was in critical, distancing terms.

But when *Sequence* writers like Anderson and Reisz became film-makers, they went into the documentary industry. In view of the attitudes they had expressed as critics this may seem odd; in fact, it was almost inevitable. The documentary cinema, whatever its shortcomings, was the easiest way for a young person to enter the cinema; the structure Grierson and his associates had created guaranteed that. If we add to this the general prestige of the British documentary film, and the fact that it is a convenient form to work in, it is not surprising that Free Cinema emerged as a documentary movement. In a sense Anderson and his associates did not choose documentary, it chose them.

The emphasis on the film's relationship to contemporary society has a prescriptive quality foreign to *Sequence*'s outlook. Since the philosophy of documentary was based on the assumption of an intimate relationship between the film-maker and his society, any alert film-maker would have been forced to consider the matter, whatever his previous ideas. In the early 1950s when the *Sequence* writers were making their first serious contacts with documentary film-making, the documentary movement was facing a crisis over its relationship with contemporary society. Documentary films were manifestly not performing their traditional function of describing contemporary society, except in limited and misleading ways. The relationship between the film-maker and society was therefore hard to avoid, particularly for the young film-maker whose view of society was likely to be less rigid than that of his seniors.

Documentary wasn't the only reason for this increasing

Every Day Except Christmas

interest in the social involvement of the film-maker. Equally strong reasons emerged from *Sequence*'s basic position. The development of the idea of 'commitment' gives a clear insight into how this occured. 'Commitment' is not mentioned in *Sequence*. It seems to have been used first by Gavin Lambert in an article in *Sight and Sound* in 1952, called 'Who wants True?' This article began as a search for some permanent standards for criticism, or as Lambert calls them 'a commitment'; but it is mostly taken up with an attack on the influence of theory and doctrine in the cinema. In his conclusion Lambert returns to the question of fixed standards and suggests that they should be grounded in the humanism he sees as a common factor in the work of Chaplin, Ford, Vigo, Dovzhenko, De Sica, Donskoi, Carné and Prévert, Clair. Fixed standards are discovered and maintained by direct reference to these great artists of the cinema:

Individual films and individual film-makers are the critic's treasure-house and the only true renovation of his spirit ... Directives for the cinema' are apt to exhaust themselves while certain film-makers and certain films remain. Response, new and renewed, to these is the only thing which can save the convert and convert the unregenerate.

This conclusion was perfectly in line with *Sequence*'s emphasis on personal response as the key part of the critical act.

Commitment then seems to have been ignored until it was forcefully discussed in Lindsay Anderson's *Sight and Sound* article of 1956, 'Stand Up! Stand Up!'. The burden of Anderson's article is that we should acknowledge our commitment and fight for it. In fact, he gives the idea of commitment an emphasis different from Lambert's. For him commitment refers to basic human values rather than to aesthetic standards. Anderson was in effect arguing that aesthetic standards emerge directly out of a person's basic values and that they do not need separate consideration. He came to this conclusion on the basis of an assumption he took absolutely for granted – that there could be no separation between form and content. 'I hope I will be pardoned if I say that I find this distinction between form and content somewhat naïf. It is the essence of poetry (in any medium) that the thing said cannot be critically distinguished from the way of saying it.'

This claim echoed the Free Cinema assertion: 'A style means an attitude. An attitude means a style.' Like Lambert, Anderson takes it for granted that the basic commitment should be to liberal humanist values. Apart from changing the emphasis in the idea of commitment, Anderson's article also changes the direction of the discussion from Lambert's interest in the nature of fixed standards to his insistence on the need to fight for them. 'Stand Up! Stand Up!' is mainly devoted to exposing writers who are evasive about their commitment.

The difference between *Sequence* and Free Cinema can be demonstrated clearly by comparing this article with an article called 'Angles of Approach' which Anderson wrote for

153

Sequence. In the *Sequence* article Anderson's approach is very close to Lambert's:

It is the critic's first duty (and in this sense we are all critics) to perceive the object of the film and to judge its success in achieving that object. This does not mean accepting every film at its own valuation; it means allowing every film to justify itself by its own standards, not by our preconceptions.

When he moved towards the territory of commitment, Anderson expressed an attitude very close to Lambert's:

'It is well done,' we may say, 'but is it worth doing?' Here it is not possible to dogmatise: but it is as well to remember that all sorts of different things are worth doing and many of them, perhaps, things we never thought of, things that fit in with no preconceived ideas of our own.

Is it possible to explain why this issue of commitment arose and why it developed in the way it did? Can Anderson's and Lambert's early formulations of the problem be reconciled with Anderson's later one?

A clue to the answer is given in the quotation Anderson cites from Lionel Trilling, at the head of this article 'Stand Up! Stand Up!'. Trilling suggests that a main objective of liberal criticism should now be to put liberal principles under some pressure. *Sequence* undoubtedly was based on liberal critical principles. But although writers like Lambert and Anderson worked within liberal assumptions, they were aware of a dilemma for liberal criticism. If the critic is to trust his own responses and be flexible and tolerant in his outlook, alert for quality in any kind of film, isn't there an inevitable drift towards relative values where everybody's critical views are given the same weight? Isn't criticism in these circumstances likely to become nothing more than a pleasant cultural diversion?

The obvious answer to the dilemma is the development of fixed principles, which both Lambert and Anderson suggest.

But such a development leads in the direction of theory and doctrine, which Anderson and Lambert as good liberals are suspicious of. 'It is a matter of fact not of opinion that the cinema is an art. *This does not call for theoretical discussion – unless, of course, you enjoy that kind of intellectual exercise.*' ('Stand Up! Stand Up!' – my italics.)

So the fixed principles they suggest are sketchy. They amount to a reaffirmation of personal response (partly responsible for creating the dilemma in the first place), and a belief in humanism. Essentially, Lambert and Anderson were trying to solve a dilemma of liberalism by re-stating the principles of liberalism. They were doing this at a time – in the early 1950s – when liberalism in general was under attack, principally as a result of the pressures generated by the cold war. Unable to explore the weaknesses in the liberal position because of his suspicion of theoretical discussion, Anderson chose to emphasise liberalism's failure of nerve and argued that its collapse was due to a lack of commitment.

The development of *Sequence* into Free Cinema should be seen as part of the general crisis of liberalism. The liberal principles developed by *Sequence* were challenged in a number of ways at very different levels: at the level of criticism through the obvious dilemmas that reliance on personal response leads to; at the level of film-making through the film-maker's difficulties in trying to express himself in a personal way within the existing commercial system; at the level of politics through the pressures of the cold war. Free Cinema was the result of this conflict, an attempt both to affirm and to adapt liberal principles in an unsympathetic cultural and political climate. For a time a solution seemed to be provided by an alliance with the New Left, hence the use of *Universities and Left Review*; but Free Cinema's suspicion of theories and ideas meant that the alliance could only be a temporary one. Some years later, Lindsay Anderson dismissed the alliance in terms that went back to *Sequence* liberalism:

We Are the Lambeth Boys

I don't regret having tried to join a New Left because it would have been very nice if the New Left had ever amounted to anything, if there really had been a radical movement we could have joined together in, both as writers, film-makers and politicians. But it did not take very long for the New Left to degenerate into a new generation of politicians or a new generation of academic theorists. And it did not take very long for us to discover that their interest in the arts was a purely propagandist one. It was only in so far as we made work that seemed to reflect what they thought to be socially acceptable that our work was in any way interesting.

After Free Cinema
The developments out of Free Cinema mark, if not the disintegration of the group, at least its withering. Free Cinema closed down on an ambiguous note:

... this is the last Free Cinema. Some will be glad, others may regret. Ourselves we feel something of each emotion. The strain of making films in this way, outside the system, is enormous, and cannot be supported indefinitely. It is not just a question of finding the money. Each time, when the films have been made, there is the same battle to be fought, for the right to *show* our work. As the madman said when he hit his head against the brick wall – 'It's nice when you stop . . .' But our feeling is not one of defeat. We have had our victories. (Free Cinema 6, programme note.)

Most of the people involved in Free Cinema moved into the feature film. The first features of Tony Richardson and Karel Reisz (*Look back in Anger*, *The Entertainer*, *A Taste of Honey* and *Saturday Night and Sunday Morning*) were obviously strongly influenced by Free Cinema attitudes. Free Cinema could claim to have played some part in making possible the whole group of contemporary social films of which Reisz's and Richardson's films were a part.

After this vein of film-making was exhausted, Free Cinema had no further perceptible influence on feature film-making. The later films of Richardson and Reisz (*Mademoiselle*, *The Sailor from Gibraltar*, *The Charge of the Light Brigade*, *Isadora*) have little or no obvious connection with Free Cinema. In criticism, the ideas developed in *Sequence* and *Sight and Sound* continued to be the basis of *Sight and Sound*'s position. (Gavin Lambert was succeeded as editor of the magazine by another *Sequence* editor, Penelope Houston.) But through the late 50s and 60s these ideas lost their vitality. This was inevitable: a wide-ranging personal response is not easy to maintain over a period of twenty years without outside stimulus. And, in any case, several of the more important writers became involved in film-making. As these included Gavin Lambert and Lindsay Anderson, the two writers who had shown the most interest in exploring the limitations of the *Sequence* approach, the position as it manifested itself in *Sight and Sound* became intellectually uncurious and not much concerned with basic principles.

At the present time, the *Sequence*/Free Cinema tradition only has any meaning for the British cinema through the work of Lindsay Anderson. Throughout his career Anderson has held to the position that the film should be the personal expression of its creator, that it should have some relevance to contemporary society, and that the supreme aesthetic value is 'poetry'. In this way his career as a film-maker has been perfectly consistent with his career as a critic.

In talking about the *Sequence*/Free Cinema tradition, one is very much talking about Anderson's career. He was an editor of *Sequence* and contributed most of its central articles. He was mainly responsible for the writing of Free Cinema propaganda and contributed the most films to its programmes. He was also a regular and important contributor to *Sight and Sound* during the 1950s. One of the weaknesses of the *Sequence*/Free Cinema tradition as an influence on British cinema was its dependence on the work of one man.

Though Free Cinema was not well enough defined or powerful enough to make a serious impact on the British cinema, the *Sequence*/Free Cinema movement might nevertheless be described as a revitalising agent. In the late 1940s *Sequence* re-established interest in the cinema as an art form when under the pressure of the thirties documentary movement it had come to be regarded as an instrument of propaganda and instruction. It broadened the range of critical interest through the discovery or re-discovery of directors like Ford, Vigo, Cocteau, Polonsky, Minnelli, Jennings and Nicholas Ray, among others. Free Cinema made the documentary film-makers more aware of the society they were living in and challenged some of the accepted conventions of documentary film-making. Through this impact it was also able to play a part in pushing the British feature film in the same direction.

The impact was not a sustained one. Under the pressure of a situation that neither its aesthetic nor its economic and social analysis of the cinema could properly cope with, the Free Cinema/*Sequence* position was modified into one simplified diagram of the cinema, a mixture of marxist and liberal attitudes – art is personal expression, personal expression is extremely difficult within a capitalist economic system, the artist's position is a very difficult one in our society.

Lindsay Anderson

In Britain, ideas developed about the cinema in the past ten years have come from different sources: the impact of *Cahiers du Cinéma*, mainly through *Movie*; underground film-making; a renewed interest in the cinema on the part of political activists; the extension of theoretical interests as a result of the impact of structuralism and semiology. In terms of ideas, Free Cinema/*Sequence* belongs to the history of the British cinema. In terms of film-making, the tradition is hardly livelier. At the present time only Lindsay Anderson has a real claim to expressing its attitudes in his work.

Filmography

The Six Free Cinema Programmes
PROGRAMME 1   5–8 February 1956
O Dreamland (1953)

Director	Lindsay Anderson
Photography	John Fletcher

Running time: 11 min
Withdrawn from distribution

Momma Don't Allow (1956)

Production	British Film Institute Experimental Film Fund
Directors	Karel Reisz, Tony Richardson
Photography	Walter Lassally
Editor/Sound	John Fletcher

With the Chris Barber Band: Chris Barber (trombone), Pat Halcox
(trumpet), Monty Sunshine (clarinet), Lonnie Donnegan (guitar), Jim Bray
(bass), Ron Bowden (drums), Ottilie Patterson (vocal)
Running time: 22 min
Distributor: 35 mm – Curzon; 16 mm – Central Booking Agency

Momma Don't Allow; Lorenza Mazzetti

Together (1953) (formerly *Glass Marbles*)

Production	British Film Institute Experimental Film Fund/Harlequin Films
Director	Lorenza Mazzetti
Story	Denis Horne
Photography	Hamid Hadari; Additional photography – Geoffrey Simpson, Walter Lassally, John Fletcher
Supervising editor	Lindsay Anderson
Editor and recordist	John Fletcher
Music	Daniel Paris

With Michael Andrews, Eduardo Paolozzi, Valy, Denis Richardson, Cecilia May
Running time: 50 min
Distributor: Connoisseur
Special mention, Cannes Film Festival, 1956

Neighbours (1953)

Director   Norman McLaren

Le Sang des Bêtes (1956)

Director   Georges Franju

On the Bowery (1956)

Director   Lionel Rogosin with the assistance of Mark
                                  Sufrin and Richard Bagely

PROGRAMME 3 – Look at Britain   25–29 May 1957
The Singing Street (1951)

Production   Norton Park Film Unit
Directors   N. McIsaac, J. T. R. Ritchie, R. Townsend
Photography   W. Geissler, R. Townsend

With pupils of Norton Park School, Edinburgh
Running time: 18 min
Distributor: British Film Institute – Amateur Section
Glasgow Film Society prize, 1952

Wakefield Express (1952)

Production	'The Wakefield Express' Ltd/Michael Robinson
Director	Lindsay Anderson
Script	Lindsay Anderson
Photography	Walter Lassally
Production assistant	John Fletcher
Commentary	Read by George Potts

Running time: 30 min
Distributor: British Film Institute

Nice Time (1957)

Production	British Film Institute Experimental Production Committee
Directors	Claude Goretta and Alain Tanner
Photography	John Fletcher
Music	Chas McDevitt Skiffle Group – Peter Cimlett (piano), Susan Baker (violin), Nancy Whiskey (vocal) and the Pete Ashton Quintet
Sound	John Fletcher

Running time: 17 min
Distributor: 35 mm – Curzon; 16 mm – Central Booking Agency

Every Day Except Christmas (1957)

Production	Graphic Films for the Ford Motor Company Ltd – The first film in their series LOOK AT BRITAIN
Producers	Leon Clore, Karel Reisz
Director	Lindsay Anderson
Script	Lindsay Anderson
Photography	Walter Lassally

The Singing Street; and Lindsay Anderson and Karel Reisz on location for *This Sporting Life*

Editor	John Fletcher
Music	Daniel Paris
Sound	John Fletcher
Assistants	Alex Jacobs, Brian Probyn, Maurice Ammar
Commentary	Spoken by Alun Owen

Running time: 47 min
Distributor: British Film Institute
Winner of the Documentary Grand Prix, Venice Film Festival, 1957

PROGRAMME 4 – Polish Voices   3–6 September 1958
Where the Devil Says Goodnight (1956)

Directors	K. Karabasz and W. Slesicki

Paragraph Zero (1956)

Director   W. Borowik

Island of Great Hope (1957)

Director   B. Pornba

The House of Old Women (1957)

Director   J. Lomnicki

Once Upon a Time (1957)

Directors   Walerian Borowczyk and Jan Lenica

Dom (1957)

Directors   Walerian Borowczyk and Jan Lenica

Two Men and a Wardrobe (1957)

Director   R. Polanski

Les Mistons (1957)

Director   François Truffaut

Le Beau Serge (1958)

Director   Claude Chabrol

PROGRAMME 6   18–22 March 1959
Food for a Blush (1959 – Extracts)

Director/Script   Elizabeth Russell
Photography   Alan Forbes
Editor   Jack Gold
Sound   Michael Tuchner

With Elizabeth Russell, Nicholas Ferguson, Felicity Innes, Brian Innes
Running time: 35 min (complete), withdrawn from distribution

Refuge England (1959)

Production   British Film Institute Experimental Film Fund
Director   Robert Vas
Script   Lazlo Marton, Robert Vas
Photography   Walter Lassally, Louis Wolfers
Music   Hungarian folk songs played on the recorder by
                    Peter Timar
Sound   Robert Allen

Tiber Molnar (young man), with Abdul Hamid Khan, Leonard Ryland, Bill
Collins
Running time: 27 min
Distributor: Connoisseur

166

Enginemen (1959)

Production	Unit Five Seven, with the assistance of the British Film Institute Experimental Film Fund
Director/Script	Michael Grigsby
Photography	Andrew Hall, Euan Halleron, Eric Harrison
Editor	Christopher Faulds
Sound	Michael Sale
Titles	Ian Thompson
Assistants	Bertram Farbridge, Jack Miller

Running time: 21 min
Distributor: British Film Institute

We Are the Lambeth Boys (1959)

Production	Graphic Films for the Ford Motor Company Ltd – the second film in their series LOOK AT BRITAIN
Executive producer	Robert Adams
Producer	Leon Clore
Director	Karel Reisz
Photography	Walter Lassally
Editor	John Fletcher
Music	Johnny Dankworth and members of the Johnny Dankworth Orchestra
Commentator	Jon Rollason
Assistants	Louis Wolfers, Raoul Sobel

Running time: 52 min
Distributor: British Film Institute
Diploma Venice Festival, 1959, Certificate of Merit Cork Festival, 1959, Grand Prix Tours Festival, 1959

167

Biographical Notes

Lindsay Anderson

Lindsay Anderson, born in Bangalore in 1923, was at Wadham College, Oxford, where he founded and edited the magazine *Sequence* (1947–52) with Karel Reisz. He wrote about films and the theatre for *Sight and Sound*, the *Observer* and *The Times*. He then made documentary films for Sutcliffe Ltd. of Wakefield: *Meet the Pioneers* (1948), *Idlers That Work* (1949), *Three Installations* (1951) and *Trunk Conveyor* (1954). In 1952 he wrote 'Making a Film' (a study of the making of Thorold Dickinson's *Secret People*), and directed the documentary *Wakefield Express*, shown in the first Free Cinema programme. He produced and played in James Broughton's *Pleasure Garden* (1952) and made with Guy Brenton the documentary *Thursday's Children* (1953) which won a Hollywood Academy Award for the best documentary of the year. Together with Karel Reisz and Tony Richardson, he launched the Free Cinema Movement, to which he contributed the independently made *O Dreamland* (1953) and *Every Day Except Christmas* (1957), and supervised the editing of *Together* (1956). During 1955 he also directed several documentaries for Basic films: for the Ministry of Agriculture *Foot and Mouth*; for the N.S.P.C.C. *A Hundred Thousand Children, The Children Upstairs, Green and Pleasant Land*, and *Henry*; and for The National Industrial Fuel Efficiency Service *£20 a Ton: Energy First*. He worked on some of the Robin Hood series of TV films from 1956–7. *March to Aldermaston* (1959) was made under the direction of a committee including Lindsay Anderson. In 1964–5 he was joint artistic director of the English Stage Company. During the making of his first major feature film *This Sporting Life* (1962) he collaborated with Richard Harris on Gogol's *Diary of a Madman*, which he directed at the Royal Court, and later theatre productions include *The Cherry Orchard* for the first

168

Chichester festival. On a visit to Warsaw in 1967, he staged Osborne's *Inadmissible Evidence*, and directed the documentary *Raz, Dwa, Trzy* (*The Singing Lesson*). Later feature films include *The White Bus* (1966) and *If* (1968) for Paramount. Lindsay Anderson also works in the theatre, principally at the Royal Court, of which he is a director, and has made television commercials. He was appointed a Governor of the B.F.I. in 1969 and resigned in 1970.

Michael Grigsby

Trained initially as a television cameraman, then worked as television director for Granada, and made film specials for that company, including *Deckie Learner* (1965), *S.S. Lusitania* and *Deep South*. He is now working as a freelance producer/director. He founded Unit Five Seven (a non-professional film unit making films in members' spare time) in 1957 and directed *Enginemen* which was shown in the Free Cinema Programme, and then *Tomorrow's Saturday* (1962). Other films made by the Unit include *Canary*, *Dirty Old Town* and *Solo*.

Lorenza Mazzetti

Born in Florence in 1929, an honours graduate of Florence University, Lorenza Mazzetti came to London in 1952 to study painting at the Slade School of Art. She persuaded the school to finance a short film from the Kafka story 'The Metamorphosis', and then directed another Kafka adaptation 'The Country Doctor', in which fellow-pupils and teachers at the Slade took part. With the support of the B.F.I. Experimental Production fund she went on to direct *Together* (which won the Prix de Recherche at Cannes in 1956) with Denis Horne and was associated with Richardson, Reisz and Anderson in the Free Cinema manifesto. Returning to Italy, she was asked to make a TV documentary about Italian youth and this won Italian Television's Gold Shield. Her principal interest is in experimental cinema and she has been working with Cesare Zavattini and other directors on a series of documentary films. At the invitation of Gian Carlo Menotti, she wrote a short play for the Spoleto festival, but this was, however, banned. She is also well known as a novelist; her first book *Il Cielo Cade* (published in England as *The Sky Folds* by Bodley Head in 1962) won the Viareggio

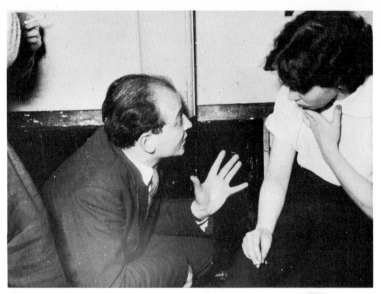

Karel Reisz directing *Momma Don't Allow*

Prize for the most outstanding Italian novel of its year; a second novel *Con Rabbia* was published by Bodley Head as *Rage* in 1965. She now lives in Rome.

Karel Reisz

Karel Reisz was born in Czechoslovakia in 1927. He wrote and compiled the book *The Technique of Film Editing* for the British Film Academy, and also worked for three years as Programmes Officer of the National Film Theatre. With Tony Richardson he directed the documentary *Momma Don't Allow*, shown in the first Free Cinema Programme in 1956. In 1956 he also became head of the Ford Motor Company's TV and Films Programme, and was co-producer on *Every Day Except Christmas*, directed by Anderson and shown in the third programme (1957). In 1958 he directed *We Are the Lambeth Boys* (shown in Free Cinema 6) which won the Grand Prix at the 1959 Tours Festival. His first feature film was

170

Saturday Night and Sunday Morning (1960) for Bryanston, and in 1963 he produced *This Sporting Life* for Woodfall. Since then his features have been shown at numerous festivals and have collected awards. They include *Night Must Fall* (1963) for M.G.M., *Morgan, A Suitable Case for Treatment* (1965) for Quintra, and *Isadora* (1968) for Universal.

Tony Richardson

Born in Shipley, Yorkshire in 1928. At Wadham College, Oxford, where he was President of OUDS. He then worked as a producer for BBC television and since has become well known as a theatrical producer, especially for the Royal Court. He was also associated with the non-profit-making London Players Group. As Associate Artistic Director of the English Stage Society he produced *Look Back in Anger*, *The Entertainer* and *Luther*, among others. He was associated with Lindsay Anderson in the Free Cinema Movement, and directed with Karel Reisz *Momma Don't Allow* in the first programme in 1956. In 1958 he founded Woodfall Films, and directed the feature *Look Back in Anger*, followed in 1959–60 by *The Entertainer*; he also produced *Saturday Night and Sunday Morning*. He directed *Sanctuary* in Hollywood in 1960, and on returning to England directed *A Taste of Honey* (1961), *The Loneliness of the Long Distance Runner* (1962) and *Tom Jones* (1963) for Woodfall. He was also executive producer on *The Girl With Green Eyes*. *The Loved One* (1965) was made for Filmways in the United States, followed by *Mademoiselle* (1965), *Sailor from Gibraltar* (1967), *The Charge of the Light Brigade* (1968), *Laughter in the Dark* (1969), and *Ned Kelly* (1970) all for Woodfall.

Elizabeth Russell

A Cambridge English graduate, she made *Food for a Blush* with Nicholas Ferguson while she was at Chelsea Art School, and later took the film to the Cork Festival. She has spent some time in America, has worked as an illustrator, researching for a projected cartoon of the *Rape of the Lock*, and has also done some teaching.

Alain Tanner/Claude Goretta

Both Swiss-born, came to England in 1956 and worked at the British Film Institute, where they made the film *Nice Time* (1957) shown in the Free Cinema programme. Alain Tanner then worked for about a year as assistant director on television documentaries, spent two years in Paris, and returned to Switzerland to make a film on Ramuz. His full-length documentary *Les Apprentis* (1964) was shown at Locarno. He went on to do more television work, and made a film on the Corbusier city in 1966, *La Vie à Chandigarh* (*A City at Chandigarh*). His latest film is the feature *Charles: Mort Ou Vif* made in 1969 in Switzerland.

Robert Vas

Born in 1931 in Budapest; spent two years at the Academy of Dramatic Arts, and worked as trainee script editor at the National Theatre in Budapest, and also at the National Puppet Theatre. He left Hungary after the collapse of the revolution in 1956 and came to England, where he worked for three years at the British Film Institute as research assistant, wrote film and television criticism, and edited television and National Coal Board Film Unit work. In 1959 he turned to making documentary films, *Refuge England* being the first, and later became a free-lance producer/director of documentaries for television. His documentary films include *The Vanishing Street* (1960), *Finale* (1961), *The Frontier* (1963), *Belonging* and *East of Bedlam* (1966), *The Survivors*, *The Quiet Hungarian* and *Koestler on Creativity* (1967). Since 1968 he has worked full time for BBC television: programmes include *The Golden Years of Alexander Korda* (1968), *An Artist from Moscow* (1969), and *Heart of Britain* (1970), a film about Humphrey Jennings.

Bibliography

John Grierson

BOOKS

Forsyth Hardy, H., *Grierson on Documentary*, Revised edition, Faber & Faber, 1966.
Rotha, Paul, *Rotha on Film*, Faber & Faber, 1958.
Rotha, Paul, *Documentary Film*, Fourth edition, Faber & Faber, 1964.
The Factual Film, sponsored by the Dartington Hall Trustees, and published on behalf of The Arts Enquiry by PEP (Political and Economic Planning), Oxford University Press, 1947.

PERIODICALS

Film Quarterly, *World Film News* and *Documentary News Letter*: the more important of Grierson's articles from these periodicals are included in *Grierson on Documentary*, and the sources are listed in the Appendix to that book. However, all three magazines are essential reading for a full background to the documentary movement.

Humphrey Jennings

BOOKS

Grigson, Geoffrey (ed.), *The Arts Today*, John Lane, The Bodley Head, 1935. Contains essay on the theatre by Jennings.

Foss, Hubert and Goodwin, Noël, *London Symphony, Portrait of an Orchestra, 1904–54*, Nabrett Press, 1954. (Contribution by Jennings.)
Rhode, Eric, *Tower of Babel*, Weidenfeld & Nicolson, 1966. Chapter on Jennings.

Pamphlets

Humphrey Jennings, A Tribute by John Grierson, Kathleen Raine, Basil Wright, Dilys Powell, Ian Dalrymple and John Greenwood; The Humphrey Jennings Memorial Fund Committee (obtainable from the B.F.I.).
Humphrey Jennings, the Painter, Institute of Contemporary Arts, prepared for the 1951 memorial exhibition.
Humphrey Jennings. Articles by James Merralls, Kathleen Raine, Jim Hillier; B.F.I. Publications, 1969.

PERIODICALS

Film Quarterly, Winter 1961–2. Special issue devoted to Jennings. Articles by Lindsay Anderson, Gerald Noxon, William Sansom and James Merralls.
Wright, Basil, 'Humphrey Jennings', *Sight and Sound*, vol. 19, no. 8, December 1950, p. 311.
Védrès, Nicole, 'Humphrey Jennings – A Memoir,' Lambert, Gavin, 'Jennings' Britain', *Sight and Sound*, vol. 23, no. 4, May 1951, p. 24.
Anderson, Lindsay, 'Only Connect: Some Aspects of the Work of Humphrey Jennings', *Sight and Sound*, vol. 23, no. 4, April/June 1954, p. 181.
Millar, Daniel, *'Fires were Started'*, *Sight and Sound*, vol. 38, no. 2, Spring 1969, p. 100.
Strick, Philip, 'Great Films of the Century, 11, *Fires were Started*', *Films and Filming*, vol. 7, no. 8, May 1961, p. 14.
Dand, Charles H., 'Britain's Screen Poet', *Films in Review*, vol. VI, no. 2, February 1955, p. 73.
Dalrymple, Ian, 'Humphrey Jennings OBE. A Tribute', *British Film Academy Quarterly*, no. 11, January 1951, p. 2.
Bronowski, J., 'Recollections of Humphrey Jennings', *Twentieth Century*, January 1959, p. 45.
Cinema Studies, no. 1, Spring 1967. Issue devoted to *A Diary for Timothy.*

174

Free Cinema

BOOKS

Maschler, Tom (Ed.), *Declaration*, MacGibbon & Kee, 1957. Essays by Doris Lessing, Colin Wilson, John Osborne, John Wain, Kenneth Tynan, Lindsay Anderson ('Get Out and Push'), Bill Hopkins and Stuart Holroyd.

Sussex, Elizabeth, *Lindsay Anderson*, Studio Vista, 1969.

PERIODICALS

Sequence (1946–1952) All 14 issues are of great interest. See especially: No. 2, Winter 1947, pp. 5–8, 'Angles of Approach, by Lindsay Anderson; No. 3, Spring 1948, pp. 7–10, 'A Possible Solution' by Lindsay Anderson; No. 5, Autumn 1948, pp. 8–12, 'Creative Elements' by Lindsay Anderson; No. 12, Autumn 1950, pp. 6–11, 37, 'The Director's Cinema' by Lindsay Anderson; No. 13, New Year 1951, pp. 11–13, 'Free Cinema' by A. Cooke; No. 14, New Year 1952, pp. 4–8, 'A Last Look Round' by Gavin Lambert.

Sight and Sound. All the issues 1950–58 are relevant since they contain many articles by Anderson, Reisz, Richardson and Lambert, and the magazine in general expresses the ideas first developed in *Sequence*. See especially: Vol. 21, No. 4, April–June 1952, pp. 148–51, 'Who Wants True' by Gavin Lambert; Vol. 26, No. 2, Autumn 1956, pp. 63–9, 'Stand Up! Stand Up!' by Lindsay Anderson.

Universities and Left Review. The early issues contain articles relevant to Free Cinema. The most important of these are: No. 1, Spring 1957, 'Commitment in Cinema Criticism' (reprint of 'Stand Up! Stand Up!') by Lindsay Anderson; No. 2, Summer 1957, 'Free Cinema' by Lindsay Anderson; No. 3, Winter 1957, 'A Use for Documentary' by Karel Reisz.

Cinema International, No. 16, 1967, pp. 685–90, 'Independent Cinema' – interviews with Lindsay Anderson and Karel Reisz.

Acknowledgements

Part of the research on which this book was based was carried out for diploma theses for the University of London Extra-mural Course in Film Study. We are grateful for the encouragement, helpful criticism and comment of Daniel Millar, Peter Wollen, and other colleagues and students. Also for the invaluable practical and research help provided by Edgar Anstey, Sir Arthur Elton, John Grierson, Stuart Legg, Robert Vas, Basil Wright; Mrs G. Bevans and Mrs J. Robinson of the Central Office of Information; The Imperial War Museum; Gail Naughton and Judy Strachan of the Education Department, and many other Departments of the National Film Archive and British Film Institute.

We are grateful to Messrs Faber & Faber for kind permission to include the quotations from *Grierson on Documentary* edited by H. Forsyth Hardy (1966), on pp. 2, 10, 11, 12, 14, 15, 16, 18, 20 and 21 of this book.

Stills are reproduced by courtesy of: Edgar Anstey and Basil Wright; Bassano (Camera Press), British Lion, Central Film Library, Radio Times Hulton Picture Library, Rank Organisation, Paul Rotha Collection and Warner-Pathé.